Get the Most Out of Your Canadian Government Pension!

Are you getting everything you can from the government?

The public pension system is complex and often changes, which means many people are not claiming money that they're entitled to. Could you use more money to pay your bills? Do you know all of your options for maximizing your pension? Many people missed out on government pensions because they failed to take action to maximize their benefits.

Read this book to make sure you're not missing out on benefits that could help you pay your bills.

Did you know?

- ❏ Government pensions are not automatic. You have to apply for it.
- ❏ You do not have to stop working to receive your government pension.
- ❏ You may be eligible for government pensions from Canada even if you are living abroad and have never worked in Canada.
- ❏ You may have to pay back part or all of your Old Age Security pension if your annual income is higher than a certain level. It is also known as the OAS clawback.
- ❏ Many people missed out on government pensions because they failed to take action to minimize the clawback.
- ❏ You can minimize the clawback, maximize your pension, and save taxes by following a few simple and proven strategies.

This book was written to help you get the most out of your government pensions. Inside you'll find everything you need to know about Canada's public pension system and the actions and strategies that you can take to reduce the clawback on your OAS pension. Specifically, you will learn:

- ❏ What benefits are offered, how to qualify, and how to apply for it.
- ❏ Why it is important to have an RRSP withdrawal strategy.
- ❏ Why it is important to have a tax-efficient investment strategy.
- ❏ How you can minimize the clawback, maximize your pension, and save taxes by following a few simple and proven strategies.

Read this book and start getting the money you deserve!

Canada's Public Pension System Made Simple

Revised & Updated 2017

Also by Lee Tang

Dual Momentum Trend Trading
Canada's Public Pension System Made Simple

Summary & Study Guide Series:

Brain Maker
The Gene
The Emperor of All Maladies
NeuroTribes
Brain Storms
The End of Diabetes
The End of Heart Disease
ADHD Nation
The Obesity Code
How Not to Die
Mind over Meds
A Crack in Creation
The Gene Machine
The Body Builders
Into the Gary Zone
Fat for Fuel
The Alzheimer's Solution
Healing Arthritis
Rise of the Necrofauna
We Are Our Brains
The Teenage Brain
The Better Brain Solution
The Plant Paradox
The Fountain
Resurrection Science
Sapiens
Homo Deus

The Beautiful Cure
The Diabetes Code
Brain Food
Anticancer Living
The End of Epidemics
The Rise and Fall of the Dinosaurs
10% Human
The Mind-Gut Connection
Civilization Microbia
An Elegant Defense
Cancerland
Empty Planet
The Longevity Paradox
Eat to Beat Disease
The Tangled Tree
The Body
The Spectrum of Hope
Memory Rescue
The Longevity Code
Healing Anxiety and Depression
Healing ADD/ADHD
The Telomere Miracle
The Finance Curse

For a complete list of books by Lee Tang and information about the author, visit LMTPRESS.WORDPRESS.COM.

Canada's Public Pension System

Made Simple

The Secrets to Maximizing Your Retirement Income from Government Pensions

Revised & Updated 2017

Lee Tang

 LMT Press

Title: Canada's Public Pension System Made Simple
Subtitle: The Secrets to Maximizing Your Retirement Income from Government Pensions
Author: Lee Tang
Publisher: LMT Press (lmtpress.wordpress.com)

Copyright © 2015, 2017 by Lee Tang

All rights reserved. Aside from brief quotations for media coverage and reviews, no part of this book may be reproduced or distributed in any form without the author's permission. Thank you for supporting authors and a diverse, creative culture by purchasing this book and complying with copyright laws.

Issued in print and electronic formats.
ISBN 9780994764010 (ebook)
ISBN 9781514784686 (paperback)
ISBN 9781987062915 (paperback)

Library and Archives Canada Cataloguing in Publication
Tang, Lee, 1951-, author
Canada's public pension system made simple: the secrets to maximizing your retirement income from government pensions / Lee Tang.
Includes bibliographical references and index.
1. Retirement income--Canada--Planning. 2. Pensions--Canada. 3. Finance, Personal--Canada. I. Title.

HG179.T33 2015	332.024'014	C2015-904096-5
		C2015-904097-3

To my wife, Lillian, who is the source of energy and love for everything I do, and to Andrew and Amanda: watching you grow up has been a privilege.

Disclaimer

The publisher and author make no representations or warranties regarding the accuracy or completeness of these contents and disclaim all warranties such as warranties of fitness for a particular purpose. The author or publisher is not liable for any damages. That an individual or organization is referred to in this document as a citation or source of information does not imply that the author or publisher endorses the information that the individual or organization provided. The website addresses in the book were correct at the time going to print. However, the publisher and author are not responsible for the content of third-party websites, which are subject to change.

This publication provides competent and reliable information regarding the subject covered. Its sole purpose is to assist readers in understanding the public pension system in Canada, independently of other financial issues. It will not explain every possible option for every individual, and the information provided is not intended as a substitute for complete financial planning. The author will do his best to keep the information current and accurate; however, given the ever-changing nature of the subject, no guarantee can be made on the accuracy of the information contained within.

Although every effort has been made to provide accurate and authoritative information regarding the subject covered, it is offered with the understanding the author and publisher are not engaged in rendering legal, financial, tax, or other professional advice for specific individual situations. The author and publisher make no written or oral representations or warranties of any kind, and specifically disclaim any liability incurred from the use or application of the contents of this book. Please consult with an attorney, accountant, or financial planner if you have any questions about your individual financial situation.

Contents

This Book Is For You   xi
Preface   xiii

Part One: Know Your Public Pensions

1. The Government Giveth   3
2. When You Become a Senior   9
3. When You Become Disabled   28
4. When You Die   35
5. When You Have Lived Abroad   43
6. The Government Taketh Away   49

Part Two: Know Your Employer Pensions and Personal Savings

7. Employer Pension Plans   67
8. Your Personal Tax Shelter   71

Part Three: Know the Secrets To Maximizing Your Retirement Income from Government Pensions

9. Finding Out Where You Stand   77
10. Maximizing Your Public Pensions   82
11. Applying to Specific Situations   91
12. The Grass Is Greener   96

Conclusion   100

Exhibit I Government Benefits Administration Offices 102
Exhibit II Provincial Income Supplement Programs 105
Exhibit III Documents Required by the OAS Application 107
Acronyms 109
Bibliography 110
Index 111
About the Author 114

This Book Is For You

THIS BOOK IS for you if you are:

- ❑ At or approaching retirement age wanting to discover what government benefits are available to you and how you can get the most out of it.
- ❑ A Canadian living abroad wanting to discover whether you are eligible for government pensions from Canada.
- ❑ A new immigrant to Canada wanting to know what your adoptive country's public pension system provides.
- ❑ A financial planner wanting to improve client services by getting a deeper knowledge of how to help your clients maximize income from government pensions.
- ❑ An immigration consultant wanting to improve client services by getting a deeper knowledge of how international social security agreements can help your clients qualify for public pensions.
- ❑ A human resources professional wanting to serve your employees better by understanding how public pension benefits relate to your employer's plans.
- ❑ A student of public policy wanting an in-depth understanding of the system.

This book is for anyone with a stake in Canada's public pension, and for those who assist others with retirement, disability, or death.

Preface

Retirement is undergoing dramatic change. People are living longer and spending more time in retirement. As life expectancy continues to increase, and fewer employers are offering defined benefit pension plans, people are by necessity becoming responsible for a greater share of their retirement funding. To help yourself prepare for a comfortable and sustainable retirement, you must understand where your retirement income is coming from and plan it accordingly.

Most Canadians have two sources of retirement income:

1. Canada's public pensions such as the Old Age Security program and the Canada/Quebec Pension Plan.

2. Private retirement savings such as employer pension plans, registered retirement savings plans, and other personal savings.

According to Statistics Canada, 41.2% of the total income of senior citizens in 2011 came from public pensions; 33.7% from private pensions and registered retirement savings plans; and the remaining 25% from investment income and other sources. Canada's public pension system plays an important role in your retirement finances. Understand how the system works and what you can do to get the most out of it.

Did You Know?

- ❑ Government pensions are not automatic. You must apply for it.
- ❑ You do not have to stop working to receive your government pensions.
- ❑ You may be eligible for Canadian government pensions even if you are living abroad and have never worked in Canada.
- ❑ You may have to pay back part or all of your Old Age Security pension if your annual income is higher than a certain level. It is also known as the OAS clawback.

Are You Getting Everything You Can From Your Government?

The public pension system is complex and often changes, which means many people are not claiming money that they're entitled to. According to the report of the Task Force on Financial Literacy, published in December 2010, many people missed out on government benefits they are entitled to because the rules are too complicated. They don't know who qualifies for what and how to apply. Here are examples from the report:

- ❑ Roughly 160,000 eligible seniors do not receive the Old Age Security benefit (representing almost $1 billion in benefits);
- ❑ About 150,000 eligible seniors do not receive the Guaranteed Income Supplement;
- ❑ Approximately 55,000 eligible Canadians are not receiving Canada Pension Plan benefits.

Many people missed out on government pensions because they failed to minimize their OAS clawback, although the clawback could have been reduced or eliminated had actions been taken.

About This Book

This book was written to help you get the most out of your government pensions. Inside you'll find everything you need to know about Canada's public pension system and the actions and strategies you can take to reduce the clawback on your OAS pension. Specifically, you will learn:

- ❏ What benefits are offered, how to qualify, and how to apply for it.
- ❏ Why it is important to have an RRSP withdrawal strategy.
- ❏ Why it is important to have a tax-efficient investment strategy.
- ❏ How you can minimize the clawback, maximize your pension, and save taxes by following a few simple and proven strategies.

Read this book to make sure you're not missing out on benefits that could help you pay your bills and balance your budget.

Part One

Know Your Public Pensions

Chapter 1

The Government Giveth

Canada's public pension system consists of a combination of government-sponsored programs:

- ❏ The Old Age Security program provides Canadians with a pension at age 65 if they satisfy certain residence requirements.
- ❏ The Canada/Quebec Pension Plan provides Canadian workers and their families with partial replacement of earnings in the case of retirement, disability or death.
- ❏ Provincial Income Supplement Programs provide their low-income residents with an income supplement to the Old Age Security benefits.
- ❏ The Veterans Affairs Canada Program provides qualified veterans with retirement, disability, and death benefits.

These programs help eligible Canadians answer concerns regarding how they will pay their bills when they retire, and what happens if they become disabled and cannot provide for themselves and their families.

Each program has separate eligibility requirements, procedures, and rules. Some programs require you to pay into the system to be eligible, others don't. Some benefits are paid only if you live in Canada, and others are paid anywhere in the world. Some benefits are income-tested, meaning the benefit amounts will be reduced if your income is over a certain level; others are not.

1.1 Old Age Security Program

The OAS Program is the first pillar of Canada's public pension system. The program began in 1952 when Parliament passed the Old Age Security Act to provide a universal pension for seniors over the age of 70, as long as they met certain Canadian residence requirements.

Between 1965 and 1969, the age of eligibility went down gradually from 70 to 65. In the 1970s, the government indexed pension payments to changes in the Consumer Price Index and to provide supplemental benefits to low-income pensioners.

In the late 1980s, after a prolonged period of inflation and economic stagnation, the government saw the pension system as costly and levied a special tax called "recovery tax" on OAS pensions to reduce and ultimately eliminate the OAS pension for people whose annual income exceeded a certain level. Today, the benefits of the program include:

- OAS Pension
- Guaranteed Income Supplement
- Allowance
- Allowance for the Survivor

The program is funded entirely by the general revenues of the Government of Canada. It provides a basic level of support to those with no other sources of retirement income. In 2014, the total expenditure of the program was 2.3% of GDP, with 35 billion paid in OAS pension and 10 billion in Guaranteed Income Supplement to 5.5 million seniors.

Service Canada is the administrator of the OAS program. See Exhibit I for contact information.

1.2 Canada/Quebec Pension Plan

The Canada Pension Plan (CPP) has been a mandatory contributory public pension program for Canadians since 1966. It provides insurance protection to a contributor against losing income due to retirement, disability, or death. The retirement pension replaces approximately 25 percent of the contributor's lifetime earnings, up to a maximum amount.

The plan covers virtually every person between the ages of 18 and 70 who works in Canada outside of Quebec and earns more than $3,500 per year. People between the ages of 18 and 70 who work in the Province of Quebec are covered by the Quebec Pension Plan (QPP). QPP broadly mirrors the CPP in most respects, and the operations of the two plans are coordinated between the federal and Quebec governments. The benefits of the Canada/Quebec Pension Plan include:

- Retirement Pension
- Post-Retirement Benefits
- Disability Benefit
- Survivor Benefit

The CPP/QPP are only partially funded by contributions from active workers, meaning that not all obligations are covered by past contributions. Some pensions could be paid out of tax revenues or contributions on a pay-go basis. You make contributions only on your annual earnings between a minimum and a maximum amount (these are called your pensionable earnings). As of 2015, the required contributions to the CPP are set to equal to 9.9% of the employee's pensionable earnings. The corresponding contribution rate for the QPP is 10.8%. Employer and employee will each pay half of the contribution while the self-employed pay the whole.

CPP/QPP YMPE and Contribution Rates		
January 2017	CPP	QPP
Maximum Pensionable Earnings	55,300	55,300
Basic exemption	3,500	3,500
Contribution rate	9.90%	10.80%
Maximum contribution for workers and employers	2,564.10	2,797.20
Maximum contribution for self-employed workers	5,128.20	5,594.40
Indexation rate for benefits as of 1 January 2017	1.40%	0.74%

Source: Canada/Quebec Pension Plan

The Canada Pension Plan is administered by Service Canada. The Quebec Pension Plan is administered by the Quebec Government. See Exhibit I for contact information.

1.3 Provincial Income Supplement Programs

Some Canadian provinces provide benefits to their low-income residents to supplement the income provided by the OAS program.

1.4 Veterans Affairs Canada Program

Veteran Affairs Canada provides a wide range of benefits and services to:

- Veterans
- Canadian Forces (CF) members (Regular and Reserve Force)
- Serving and discharged members of the Royal Canadian Mounted Police (RCMP)
- Certain civilians; and their families.

1.5 Key Points

- OAS program is a non-contributory retirement income program funded out of the general revenues of the Government of Canada. It provides four types of benefits—the OAS pension, the GIS, the Allowance, and the Allowance for the Survivor.
- Canada Pension Plan is a mandatory contributory public pension program for a person between the ages of 18 and 70 who works in Canada outside of Quebec. It provides insurance protection to a contributor against losing income due to retirement, disability, or death.
- Quebec Pension Plan is similar to the Canada Pension Plan but only for a person who works in Quebec.

- CPP/QPP offers four types of benefits - retirement pension, post-retirement benefits, disability, and survivors.
- Some Canadian provinces provide benefits to their low-income residents to supplement the income provided by the OAS program.
- Veterans Affairs Canada provides income supplements and disability benefits to qualified veterans.

1.6 Resources

- Old Age Security Program (http://www.servicecanada.gc.ca/oas)
- Canada Pension Plan (http://www.servicecanada.gc.ca/cpp)
- Quebec Pension Plan (http://www.rrq.gouv.qc.ca/en/programmes/regime_rentes/Pages/regime_rentes.aspx)
- Veterans Affairs Canada (http://www.veterans.gc.ca)

Chapter 2

When You Become a Senior

When you become a senior, you may be eligible for a retirement pension from the public pension system. Your spouse and the dependent child may also be eligible for benefits when you qualify for a public pension and have little or no income. See below.

2.1 Retirement Pension

As you reach retirement age, you may be eligible for a retirement pension from one or more of these programs.

2.1.1 OAS Pension

An OAS pension is a monthly taxable benefit payable to an individual who meets age and Canadian residence requirements.

Eligibility

To be eligible for an OAS pension, you must have one of these requirements:

(A) If you live in Canada, you must:

- ❏ Be age 65 or older.
- ❏ Be a legal resident or a Canadian citizen.
- ❏ Have lived in Canada for at least 10 years after attaining age 18.

(B) If you live abroad, you must:
- ❏ Be age 65 or older.
- ❏ Be a legal resident or a Canadian citizen when you left Canada.
- ❏ Have lived in Canada for at least 20 years after attaining age 18.

If you meet one of the above requirements, you can receive an OAS pension even if you are still working or have never worked. If neither of the above applies to you, you may still qualify for an OAS pension if you have lived in one of the countries with which Canada has established an international social security agreement (see Chapter 5).

Your OAS pension will *stop* if you leave Canada for over 6 consecutive months unless you have lived in Canada for at least 20 years after attaining age 18. Your pension payment will resume once you return to Canada. Your pension will be *suspended* if you are imprisoned in a federal penitentiary for two years or longer. Your pension will resume upon your release.

Note: Beginning April 2023 the age of eligibility for the OAS pension will gradually increase from 65 to 67 over six years, with full implementation by January 2029. This change will affect those born in 1958 and later.

Benefits

As of July 1 2017, the monthly payment for those entitled to the full pension is $583.74. The pension is adjusted for inflation every quarter. You may qualify for the full pension if you satisfy one of these requirements:

- ❏ You have lived in Canada for at least 40 years after attaining age 18.
- ❏ You were born before July 1, 1952, and you lived in Canada when you reached age 25 or had a valid immigration visa on July 1, 1977, and you lived in Canada for the ten years immediately prior to approving the pension.

If you do not qualify for the full pension, you may qualify for a prorated partial pension based on your length of residence in Canada. For example, if you have lived in Canada for 30 years after attaining age 18, then you will be qualified to receive a pension equal to 75% (30 divided by 40) of the full pension.

The OAS Recovery Tax (to be discussed in chapter 6) requires all higher-income pensioners to repay their OAS pension at 15% of their income above a certain threshold. This is the *OAS clawback*. The income threshold for the OAS Recovery Tax is indexed annually to changes in the Consumer Price Index. In 2017, the threshold amount (including the OAS pension) wss $74,788.

How to Apply

To receive an OAS pension, you must apply for it. The earliest you can apply is 11 months before your 65th birthday. You can apply online using the My Service Canada Account service, or by mail. See the Resource section for more information.

You may delay receiving your pension by up to 60 months. If you do that, your pension will go up by 0.6% per month for each month you delay receiving your pension. So, if you postpone your retirement to age 70, your pension will be 36% higher. But if you delay receiving your OAS pension, you will not be eligible for the GIS (see section 2.1.2) and your spouse will not be eligible for the Allowance (see section 2.2.1) for the period you are delaying your OAS pension.

Documents Required with the Application
- Proof of date of birth
- Proof of Canadian Legal Status (see Exhibit III)
- Proof of Residence History (see Exhibit III)

2.1.2 OAS Guaranteed Income Supplement

The Guaranteed Income Supplement (GIS) is a monthly non-taxable benefit payable to OAS pension recipients living in Canada with little or no other income. Nearly one-third of all OAS recipients in Canada qualify for and receive the GIS.

Eligibility

To be eligible for the GIS benefit, you must meet these requirements:

- You are living in Canada.
- You are receiving an OAS pension.
- Your annual income (or with a couple, your combined income) is lower than the established maximum annual income.

Your annual income is defined as your income as reported on Line 234 of the federal Income Tax Return excluding income from your OAS pension, GIS and Allowance benefits.

Sponsored immigrants are not eligible to receive the GIS during their sponsorship period unless they have 10 years of residence in Canada after attaining age 18 or the sponsorship agreement ends because the sponsor

- Suffers personal bankruptcy.
- Is imprisoned for over six months.
- Is convicted of abusing the sponsored immigrant.
- Dies.

Non-sponsored immigrants may be eligible to receive the GIS based on the number of years of residence in Canada after attaining age 18. Your GIS will *stop* if

- You leave Canada for over 6 consecutive months.
- You are imprisoned in a federal penitentiary for two years or longer.
- You have not filed an income tax return with the Canada Revenue Agency by April 30, or if, by the end of June each year, Service Canada has not received the information about your net income (or in the case of a couple, your combined net income) for the previous year.
- Your annual income (or with a couple, your combined annual income) is above the maximum annual income.

Benefits

The GIS benefit is adjusted for inflation every quarter and is based on the length of your residence in Canada, marital status, and income. You must have lived in Canada for at least 10 years after attaining age 18 to receive the maximum benefit. A prorated benefit is payable if you have less than 10 years of residence. The table below shows the maximum monthly GIS payable to an OAS recipient.

GIS Benefit Rates (June - September, 2017)		
Family Status	Max Monthly Payment	Max Annual Income Limit
Single, widowed or divorced pensioner	871.86	17,688 (individual income)
Couple, spouse is also an OAS recipient	524.85	23,376 (combined income)
Couple, spouse is not receiving OAS benefits	871.86	42,384 (combined income)
Couple, spouse getting allowance	524.85	42,384 (combined income)

Source: Service Canada

How to Apply

You must receive an OAS pension to qualify for the GIS benefits. If you are delaying your OAS pension, you will not be eligible for the GIS benefit even though you meet the other requirements.

If you are already a recipient of the OAS pension, but not the GIS benefit, you can apply online using the My Service Canada Account service, or by mail. See the Resource section for more information.

If you are receiving the GIS, your benefits will be renewed automatically each year if as you remain eligible and file an annual income tax return on time. If you do not file your return on time, you will receive a renewal form from Service Canada. If you do not renew your application for the GIS in the spring by either filing your income tax return or completing a Renewal of Guaranteed Income Supplement form, your GIS benefit will stop in July of that year.

2.1.3 CPP/QPP Retirement Pension

The Canada/Quebec Pension Plan Retirement Pension provides a monthly taxable benefit to an individual who meets the eligibility requirements.

Eligibility

You are eligible to apply for a retirement pension when you are age 60 or over if you have made at least one contribution to the plan, regardless of whether you have stopped working or not. The standard age to receive the pension is 65. However, you can take a permanently reduced pension as early as age 60 or take a permanently increased pension after age 65.

Here are the things to consider in deciding when to apply for a retirement pension:

- Your pension depends on your contribution and earnings history.
- If you start your CPP/QPP pension before 65, your pension will be reduced by 0.6 percent a month for each month between the age of 65 and the age your pension commences. So, if you take early retirement at age 60, your pension will be 36% lower.
- If you delay receiving your pension until after age 65, your pension will go up by 0.7% per month for each month you delay receiving your pension. So, if you postpone your retirement to age 70, your pension will be 42% higher.
- If you work while receiving your CPP/QPP retirement pension, you can increase your retirement income by continuing to contribute to the plan until you reach age 70.

Benefits

As of January 1, 2017, the maximum pension amount is $1,114.17 per month. This amount is indexed to the changes in the Consumer

Price Index on a calendar year basis. Your initial retirement pension depends on how much you have contributed, how long you have contributed and the age at which you want to start the retirement pension payment. In calculating your pension benefits, 17 percent of your lowest earnings years (up to 8 years) are removed from the calculation. There is also an adjustment for the years when a parent was at home with children under the age of seven. This is called the *Child Rearing Provision*.

How to Apply

To receive the CPP/QPP retirement pension, you must apply for it. You can apply online or by mail after completing an application form. See the Resource section for more information.

2.1.4 CPP/QPP Post-Retirement Benefits

If you continue working and contributing to the CPP while you are receiving a retirement pension from the plan, you can receive a Post-Retirement Benefit (PRB). The corresponding benefit in the QPP is called Retirement Pension Supplements (RPS).

Eligibility

You might be eligible if you are:

- 60 to 70 years of age.
- Working and contributing to the CPP/QPP.
- Receiving a retirement pension from the CPP/QPP.

To get this benefit, you and your employer must contribute to the plan. If you are self-employed, you must pay both the employee and the employer portions of the contributions. Contributions are mandatory if you are younger than 65, and optional if you are between 65 and 70. You will stop contributing to the plan after age 70.

Benefits

The maximum PRB for a single year is equal to 1/40th of the maximum CPP retirement pension. If you contribute less than the maximum, the year's PRB will be proportional to your contribution. For example, contributing half of the maximum will generate 50 percent of the maximum PRB.

How to Apply

You don't have to apply. If you are eligible, it will be paid to you automatically.

2.1.5 Provincial Income Supplement Programs

Some Canadian provinces provide benefits to their low-income residents to supplement the income provided by the OAS program. Here are the programs currently available. See Exhibit II for more information on these programs.

- **British Columbia** — The British Columbia Senior's Supplement provides an income supplement for eligible senior residents if his or her income level is below the level guaranteed by the Province. The maximum monthly benefit is $49.30 for single seniors and $120.50 for senior couples.

- **Alberta** — The Alberta Seniors Benefit program is based on income. As of January 1, 2017, a single senior with an annual income of $27,300 or less, and senior couples with a combined annual income of $44,335 or less are eligible for a benefit.

- **Saskatchewan** — The Saskatchewan Seniors Income Plan provides a monthly supplement to seniors who have little or no income other than the federal OAS pension and the Guaranteed Income Supplement. The maximum income benefit is $270 per month.

- ❏ **Manitoba** — The Manitoba 55 PLUS Program provides quarterly benefits to low-income Manitobans who are age 55 or older.

- ❏ **Ontario** — The Ontario G.A.I.N.S. (Guaranteed Annual Income System) program provides benefit payments to seniors with little or no income other than the federal OAS pension and the Guaranteed Income Supplement.

- ❏ **New Brunswick** — The New Brunswick Low-Income Seniors Benefit Program provides an annual benefit of $400 to New Brunswick residents receiving federal OAS pensions.

- ❏ **Nova Scotia** — Under the Nova Scotia Seniors Provincial Tax Refund Program, seniors receiving the federal Guaranteed Income Supplement benefits will get a refund of their provincial income tax.

- ❏ **Newfoundland and Labrador** — Newfoundland and Labrador Low-Income Seniors' Benefit is a refundable tax credit for low-income seniors.

- ❏ **Yukon** — The Yukon Low-Income Seniors Income Supplement Program provides a monthly benefit to low-income seniors. The program is automatically available to eligible seniors receiving the federal OAS pension, the Guaranteed Income Supplement or the allowance benefits.

- ❏ **Northwest Territories** — The Northern Territories Senior Citizens Supplementary Benefit Program provides a monthly benefit to low-income seniors. The program is automatically available to eligible seniors receiving the federal OAS pension, the Guaranteed Income Supplement or the allowance benefits.

- **Nunavut** — The Nunavut Senior Citizen Supplementary Benefit (SCSB) provides a monthly benefit of $200.00 to low-income seniors in Nunavut.
- **Quebec/Prince Edward Island** — No specific social security supplement programs are listed.

2.1.6 War Veterans Allowance

The War Veterans Allowance (WVA) provides a monthly financial assistance to help low-income Veterans and their Survivors meet their basic needs. The program also provides income support to eligible civilians who worked closely with the CAF during the Second World War.

Eligibility

Eligibility is based on wartime service as either a Veteran or a Civilian. Other eligibility requirements include age, health, income, and residency.

- Service
  - Veterans (including Merchant Navy Veterans) of the Second World War or the Korean War; Allied Veterans of the Second World War or the Korean War who meet residency status (see below); or
  - Certain civilians who served during the Second World War.
- **Age or Health** — Male applicants must be 60 years of age and female applicants must be 55. WVA may be awarded at an earlier age to an applicant who is:
  - Unable to work due to a physical or mental disability;
  - Unable, and unlikely to be able to support him/herself due to a physical or mental disability and economic handicap;

- Unable to support him/herself because of the need to provide care for a dependent child living at home; or
- An orphan.

☐ **Income** — WVA is an income-tested benefit. Income is assessed using the same standard for the Guaranteed Income Supplement, which is based on the Income Tax Act. Annual income exemptions, such as the casual earnings exemption and the interest exemption, are available and can be considered during your assessment.

☐ **Residency Status**
- You must have lived in Canada prior to your enlistment with an Allied Force; or
- You must have lived in Canada for 10 years (need not be consecutive) since your service with an Allied Force.

Benefits

War Veterans Allowance is payable monthly. The amount depends on income, family status and the number of qualified dependents. As of 2017, the maximum monthly payment is $1,559.45 for the veteran or survivor.

How to Apply

You must be living in Canada (and have been living in Canada for at least 12 consecutive months) when you apply for WVA. You can call 1-866-522-2122 (toll-free) and ask them to mail you the form.

2.2 Family Benefits for Low-Income Pensioners

If you are eligible for government pensions and you have little or no income, your spouse and the dependent child may be eligible for these benefits.

2.2.1 OAS Allowance

Allowance is a monthly non-taxable benefit payable to the spouse or common-law partner of GIS recipients.

Eligibility

To be eligible for the Allowance benefit, you must meet the following:

- You are aged 60 to 64.
- Your spouse or common-law partner receives an OAS pension and is eligible for the GIS.
- You are a Canadian citizen or a legal resident.
- You are living in Canada and have lived in Canada for at least 10 years after attaining 18.
- Your annual income (or with a couple, the combined income) is less than the established maximum annual income.

You may also qualify for the Allowance

- If your spouse or common-law partner is imprisoned.
- If you have not resided in Canada for at least 10 years since you turned 18, but you have resided or worked in a country with a social security agreement with Canada.

Sponsored immigrants are not eligible to receive the Allowance during the sponsorship period unless they have 10 years of residence in Canada after attaining age 18 or the sponsorship agreement ends because the sponsor:

- Suffers personal bankruptcy.
- Is imprisoned for over six months
- Is convicted of abusing the sponsored immigrant.
- Dies.

Non-sponsored immigrants may be eligible to receive the Allowance based on the number of years of residence in Canada after attaining age 18.

Your Allowance will stop if

- You become eligible for OAS benefits at age 65.
- You leave Canada for over 6 consecutive months.
- You are imprisoned in a federal penitentiary for two years or longer.
- You have not filed an income tax return with the Canada Revenue Agency by April 30, or if, by the end of June each year, Service Canada has not received any information about your net income (or with a couple, your combined net income) for the previous year.
- Your net income (or with a couple, your combined net income) is above the maximum annual income.
- You are divorced or separated from your spouse.
- Your spouse is no longer eligible for the GIS.
- Your spouse or common-law partner dies (you may be eligible for the allowance for the survivor).

Note: Starting in April 2023, the age of eligibility for the Allowance will gradually increase from 60 to 62, with full implementation by January 2029.

Benefits

As of July 2017, the maximum allowance payable is $1,108.59 per month, and your combined income must not exceed $32,736. The allowance benefit is adjusted every quarter and is based on the length of your residence in Canada, family status, and income. You must have lived in Canada for at least 10 years after attaining age 18 to receive the full benefit. A pro-rated amount is payable if you have less than 10 years of residence.

How to Apply

You can apply no earlier than 11 months before your 60th birthday. If you have reached age 60, send your application soon so you will lose no payments. You can apply online using the My Service Canada Account service, or by mail. See the Resource section for more information.

Documents Required by the Application:
- Proof of date of birth
- Proof of Marital Status
- Proof of Canadian Legal Status (see Exhibit III)
- Proof of Residence History (see Exhibit III)

If you are receiving the Allowance, your benefits will be renewed automatically each year as long as you remain eligible and file an annual income tax return on time. If you do not file your return on time, you will receive a renewal form from Service Canada. If you do not renew your application for the Allowance benefit in the spring by either filing your income tax return or completing a renewal form, your Allowance benefit will stop in July of that year.

2.2.2 Provincial Income Supplement Programs

If you are eligible for the GIS benefit under the OAS program, your spouse may also be eligible for the provincial income supplement programs under some provinces. See Exhibit II for details on the programs.

2.2.3 War Veterans Allowance

If you are eligible for the WVA, your spouse and the dependent child may also qualify for the WVA.

Eligibility
See section 2.1.6.

Benefits

As of 2017, the maximum monthly payment is $764.56 for the spouse and $345.76 for each dependent child.

How to Apply

You must be living in Canada (and have been living in Canada for at least 12 consecutive months) when you apply for WVA. You can call 1-866-522-2122 (toll-free) and ask them to mail you the form.

2.3 Key Points

2.3.1 Retirement Pensions

- Eligibility for the OAS pension depends on how long you have lived in Canada.
- The OAS benefits are 'income-tested.' This means that once your income exceeds a certain level, you must pay back part or all of your benefits.
- Your Guaranteed Income Supplement benefit will be renewed automatically every year if you remain eligible and file an income tax return on time.
- The CPP/QPP retirement benefits can start anytime between the age of 60 and 70, with corresponding adjustments to benefits.
- Some Canadian provinces provide an income supplement to their low-income senior residents.
- Veterans Affairs Canada provides qualified low-income veterans with a monthly income called War Veterans Allowance to meet basic needs.

2.3.2 Family Benefits

- These family benefits are available to assist low-income pensioners to feed their families.
- The spouse of a GIS recipient may be eligible for the OAS allowance benefit if she meets her age, Canadian residence, and income requirements.
- Your allowance benefit will be renewed automatically every year if you remain eligible and file an income tax return on time.
- The spouse of a GIS recipient may be eligible for provincial income supplement benefits.
- War Veterans Allowance provides monthly benefits to the spouse and dependent children of a qualified low-income veteran.

2.4 Resources

2.4.1 Old Age Security Pension

- Old Age Security payment amounts (http://www.servicecanada.gc.ca/eng/services/pensions/oas/payments/index.shtml)
- Service Canada Online Services and Forms (http://www.servicecanada.gc.ca/eng/online/index.shtml)
- Sign-In Page for My Service Canada Account (http://www.servicecanada.gc.ca/eng/online/mysca.shtml)
- Application for the Old Age Security pension (ISP3000) (http://www.servicecana-

da.gc.ca/cgi-bin/search/eforms/index.cgi?app=profile&form=isp3000)

2.4.2 Guaranteed Income Supplement

- Application for the Guaranteed Income Supplement (ISP3025) (http://www.servicecanada.gc.ca/fi-if/index.jsp?app=prfl&frm=isp3025&lang=eng)

- Application for Allowance or Allowance for the Survivor (ISP3008) (http://www.servicecanada.gc.ca/fi-if/index.jsp?app=prfl&frm=isp3008&lang=eng)

- Application for the Renewal of GIS, Allowance or Allowance for the Survivor (ISP3026) (http://www.servicecanada.gc.ca/fi-if/index.jsp?app=prfl&frm=isp3026&lang=eng)

2.4.3 Application for CPP Retirement Pension

- Application for a CPP Retirement Pension online (http://www.servicecanada.gc.ca/eng/services/pensions/cpp/retirement/apply.shtml)

- <u>Application for a CPP Retirement Pension by mail (ISP1000)</u> (http://www.servicecanada.gc.ca/fi-if/index.jsp?app=prfl&frm=isp1000&lang=eng)

- Application for Pension Sharing of CPP Retirement Pensions (ISP1002) (http://

www.servicecanada.gc.ca/fi-if/index.jsp?
app=prfl&frm=isp1002&lang=eng)

- Application for CPP Child Rearing Provision (ISP1640) (http://www.servicecanada.gc.ca/fi-if/index.jsp?app=prfl&frm=isp1640&lang=eng)

2.4.4 Application for QPP Retirement Pension

- Application for QPP Retirement Pension online (http://www.rrq.gouv.qc.ca/en/services/services_en_ligne/regime_rentes_quebec/Pages/rente_retraite.aspx)

- Application for QPP Retirement Pension by mail (http://www.rrq.gouv.qc.ca/SiteCollectionDocuments/www.rrq.gouv.qc/Anglais/formulaires/regime_rentes/Retraite/B001_en.pdf)

- Application for QPP Retirement Pension Sharing Between Spouses (http://www.rrq.gouv.qc.ca/SiteCollectionDocuments/www.rrq.gouv.qc/Anglais/formulaires/regime_rentes/Retraite/RRQ060_en.pdf)

2.4.5 Veterans Affairs Canada

- Application for War Veterans Allowance (http://www.veterans.gc.ca/eng/forms/document/429)

Chapter 3

When You Become Disabled

If you become disabled, you may be eligible for a disability pension, and your spouse and children may be eligible for family benefits from the public pension system.

3.1. Disability Pension

If disabled, you may be eligible for a disability pension from the Canada/Quebec pension plan and/or the Veterans Affairs Canada program. See below.

3.1.1 CPP/QPP Disability Benefit

The CPP/QPP Disability Benefit is a monthly benefit available to people who have contributed to the plan and whose disability prevents them from working at any job regularly. A disability pension converts to a retirement pension at age 65.

Eligibility

If you become disabled prior to age 65 and are not receiving a retirement pension from the plan, you will be eligible for a disability benefit provided that you have contributed for:

- at least 4 of the past 6 years, or
- at least 3 of the past 6 years if you have contributed for at least 25 years.

To qualify for the benefit, your disability must be both **severe** (you cannot do ANY job) and **prolonged** (meaning for an indefinite duration or likely to result in your death).

Benefits

The disability pension is the sum of a flat-rate portion and an earnings-related portion. As of January 2017, the maximum disability pension amount is $1,290.81 per month.

How to Apply

You must apply in writing. Print out the main application form, the consent forms, and any other necessary forms from the application kit for disability benefits, and mail them to the address indicated on the form.

3.1.2 Veterans Affairs Disability Pension

If you are a veteran, you may qualify for a disability pension.

Eligibility

You may qualify for a disability pension if you have a medical disability related to your service and you are:

- Canadian Forces (CF) Veteran or a Merchant Navy Veteran of the First or Second World War or the Korean War;
- A current or former member of the Regular or Reserve Force; or
- A civilian who served in support of the Armed Forces during wartime.

Benefits

The pension is based on an assessment of the relationship between service and disability. As of January 2017, the maximum monthly pension payable on the highest assessment was $2,733.47. Additional amounts are also payable to the spouse and dependent children of the disabled veteran.

How to Apply

Obtain and complete a VAC application for Disability Benefits (http://www.veterans.gc.ca/eng/forms/document/493) package. Mail the applications, including supporting documents, to:

Veterans Affairs Canada
PO Box 6000, Matane, QC G4W 0E4

3.2 Family Benefits for the Disabled

When disabled, your dependent child may be eligible for a monthly benefit from the Canada/Quebec pension plan. If you are also a veteran, your spouse and dependent children may also be eligible for monthly benefits from the VAC program. See below.

3.2.1 CPP/QPP Disability Benefit for Child

If you are eligible for the CPP/QPP disability benefit, your children may be eligible for a child benefit. If both parents are eligible for disability, the child's benefit will be paid twice (by each parent).

Eligibility

If the contributor is eligible for disability benefits:

- ❑ Children under the age of 18, or between the ages of 18 and 25 and attending school full-time are eligible for child benefit under the CPP.

- ❑ Children under the age of 18 (only) are eligible for child benefit under the QPP.

Benefits

The child's benefit is a flat rate per child. As of January 2017, the amount of a child's benefit is $241.02 per month.

How to Apply

You must apply in writing. See the Resources section for the application forms.

3.2.2 Veterans Affairs Disability Pension for Spouse and Child

If you are eligible for VA disability pension, your spouse and dependent children may qualify for benefits under the program.

Eligibility

Your spouse and dependent child may qualify for a disability pension if you have a medical disability related to your service and you are:

- ❏ Canadian Forces (CF) Veteran or a Merchant Navy Veteran of the First or Second World War or the Korean War;
- ❏ A current or former member of the Regular or Reserve Force; or
- ❏ A civilian who served in support of the Armed Forces during wartime.

Benefits

The pension is based on an assessment of the relationship between service and disability. As of 2017, the maximum pension payable to the spouse of the disability pension is $683.37 per month on the highest assessment. Additional amounts are $355.35 per month for the first child, $259.68 per month for the second child, and $205.01 per month for each additional child.

How to Apply

Obtain and complete a VAC application for Disability Benefits package (http://www.veterans.gc.ca/eng/forms/document/493). Mail the applications, including supporting documents, to:

Veterans Affairs Canada
PO Box 6000, Matane, QC G4W 0E4

3.3 Key Points

3.3.1 Benefits for the Disabled

- ❏ There is a minimum contribution requirement for a contributor to be eligible for the CPP/QPP disability benefit.

- ❏ To qualify for the CPP/QPP disability benefits, your disability must be both severe (you are unable to do ANY job) and prolonged (meaning for an indefinite duration or likely to result in your death).

- ❏ VA Disability Pension Program provides monthly benefits to a veteran with a service-related medical disability.

3.3.2 Benefits for the Family of the Disabled

- ❏ If the CPP/QPP contributor is eligible for the CPP/QPP disability benefits, his or her dependent children may be eligible for the child benefit

- ❏ VA Disability Pension Program provides monthly benefits to the spouse and dependent children of a qualified veteran.

3.4 Resources

3.4.1 Canada Pension Plan

- Application For CPP Disability Benefits (ISP1151) (http://www.servicecanada.gc.ca/fi-if/index.jsp?app=prfl&frm=isp1151)

- Consent for Service Canada to Obtain Personal Information (ISP2502) (http://www.servicecanada.gc.ca/fi-if/index.jsp?app=prfl&frm=isp2502&lang=eng)

- Application for Benefits for children of Disabled Contributor under the age of 18 (ISP1152) (http://www.servicecanada.gc.ca/fi-if/index.jsp?app=prfl&frm=isp1152&lang=eng)

- Application for a CPP Child's Benefit (ISP1400) (http://www.servicecanada.gc.ca/fi-if/index.jsp?app=prfl&frm=isp1400&lang=eng)

- Declaration of Attendance at School or University (ISP1401) (http://www.servicecanada.gc.ca/fi-if/index.jsp?app=prfl&frm=isp1401&lang=eng)

3.4.2 Quebec Pension Plan

- [Application for QPP Disability Benefits](http://www.rrq.gouv.qc.ca/SiteCollectionDocuments/www.rrq.gouv.qc/Anglais/formulaires/regime_rentes/invalidite/B071_en.pdf) (http://www.rrq.gouv.qc.ca/SiteCollec-tionDocuments/www.rrq.gouv.qc/Anglais/formulaires/regime_rentes/invalidite/B071_en.pdf)

3.4.3 Veterans Affairs Disability Pension

- [VAC application for Disability Benefits package](http://www.veterans.gc.ca/eng/forms/document/493) (http://www.veterans.gc.ca/eng/forms/document/493)

Chapter 4

When You Die

If you die, your estate will receive a lump-sum death benefit, while your spouse and the dependent child may be eligible for a monthly benefit. See below.

4.1 OAS Allowance for the Survivor

Allowance for the Survivor is a monthly non-taxable benefit available to eligible low-income resident Canadians aged between 60 and 64 who are widows or widowers.

Eligibility

To be eligible for the allowance for the Survivor benefit, you must meet the following:

- ❏ You are aged 60 to 64.
- ❏ You are a Canadian citizen or a legal resident.
- ❏ You are living in Canada and have lived in Canada for at least 10 years since the age of 18.
- ❏ Your spouse or common-law partner has died, and you have not remarried or entered a common-law relationship.

- Your annual income is less than the established maximum annual income.

Sponsored immigrants are not eligible to receive the Allowance for the Survivor during the sponsorship period unless they have 10 years of residence in Canada after attaining age 18 or the sponsorship agreement ends because the sponsor:

- Suffers personal bankruptcy.
- Is imprisoned for over six months.
- Is convicted of abusing the sponsored immigrant.
- Dies.

Non-sponsored immigrants may be eligible to receive the Allowance for the Survivor based on the number of years of residence in Canada after attaining age 18. Your Allowance for the Survivor will *stop* if

- You become eligible for OAS benefits at age 65.
- You leave Canada for over 6 consecutive months.
- You are imprisoned in a federal penitentiary for two years or longer.
- You have not filed an income tax return with the Canada Revenue Agency by April 30, or if, by the end of June each year, Service Canada has not received any information about your net income (or with a couple, your combined net income) for the previous year.
- Your net income (or with a couple, your combined net income) is above the maximum annual income.
- You have remarried.

Note: Starting in April 2023, the age of eligibility for the Allowance for the Survivor will gradually increase from 60 to 62, with full implementation by January 2029.

Benefits

As of January 1, 2017, the maximum allowance payable is $1,321.46 per month, and your annual income must not exceed $23,832. The Allowance for the Survivor benefit is adjusted every quarter and is based on your length of residence in Canada, family status, and income. You must have lived in Canada for at least 10 years after attaining age 18 to receive the full benefit. A pro-rated amount is payable if you have less than 10 years of residence.

How to Apply

You can apply no earlier than 11 months before your 60th birthday. If you have reached age 60, send your application soon so you will lose no payments. You can apply online using the My Service Canada Account service, or by mail. See the Resource section for more information.

If you are receiving the Allowance for the Survivor, your benefits will be renewed automatically each year, as long as you remain eligible and file an annual income tax return on time. If you do not file your return on time, you will receive a renewal form from Service Canada. If you do not renew your application for the allowance benefit in the spring by either filing your income tax return with the Canada Revenue Agency or completing a renewal form, your allowance benefit will stop in July of that year.

Documents Required by the Application

- ❏ Proof of date of birth
- ❏ Proof of Marital Status
- ❏ Proof of Canadian Legal Status
- ❏ Proof of Residence History
- ❏ Proof of your spouse's date of death
- ❏ Proof of your marriage

4.2 CPP/QPP Survivor Benefits

When you die, a survivor benefit is payable to the estate, the spouse and/or dependent children.

Eligibility
To be eligible for the benefit, you must have contributed for at least 3 years.

Benefits
- **Lump-sum Death Benefit**—the lump-sum death benefit (maximum $2,500) is payable to your estate.
- **Pension for Surviving Spouse**—The survivor pension benefit is a monthly pension paid to the surviving spouse of the deceased contributor. The survivor pension depends on the age of the survivor on the date of the contributor's death, the survivor's disability status, and dependent children. If both a survivor and retirement benefit are payable, the survivor benefit is reduced. The survivor pension benefit continues even if the surviving spouse remarries. If he or she is widowed a second time, only one survivor pension will be paid. It will be the larger of the two. As of January 2017, the maximum survivor pension paid to the spouse is $604.32 when the survivor is younger than 65 and $668.50 per month when the survivor is 65 or older.
- **Pension for Dependent Children**—Children under the age of 18 are eligible for the child pension. The CPP (but not the QPP) extends the benefits to children between the ages of 18 and 25 and attending school full-time. As of January 2017, the child pension is $241.02 per month.

How to Apply

You can apply online or by mail. See the Resources section for more information.

4.3 War Veterans Allowance

Surviving spouses, surviving common-law partners or orphans may qualify for WVA if the deceased Veterans or civilians had the required war service. A survivor's pension will be paid to the surviving spouse commencing one year from the time of death. The pensioner's benefits will continue in full for the first year. If the pensioner was receiving a pension of 48% or greater, the survivor may have a full survivor's pension. If the pensioner was receiving a pension between the 5% and 47% rate, the survivor would receive one-half of the Disability Pension paid to the pensioner. Surviving spouses or common-law partners who remarry will continue to receive the survivor's pension. Children and other qualified dependents may also qualify for benefits following a pensioner's death.

How to Apply

You must be living in Canada (and have been living in Canada for at least 12 consecutive months) when you apply for WVA. You can call 1-866-522-2122 (toll-free) and ask them to mail you the form.

4.4 Key Points

- ❑ The surviving spouse of a GIS recipient may be eligible for the Allowance for the Survivor benefit if she meets her age, Canadian residence, and income requirements.

- ❑ Your allowance for the survivor benefit will be renewed automatically every year if you remain eligible and file an income tax return on time.

- CPP/QPP provides three types of survivor benefits - a lump sum payable to the estate, a monthly pension payable to the surviving spouse, and a monthly payment to the dependent children.
- To be eligible for the CPP/QPP Survivor benefits, you must have contributed for at least 3 years.
- War Veterans Allowance provides monthly benefits for the surviving spouse and dependent children of a qualified veteran.

4.5 Resources

4.5.1 Application for OAS Survivor Benefits

- Application for Allowance or Allowance for the Survivor (ISP3008) (http://www.servicecanada.gc.ca/fi-if/index.jsp?app=prfl&frm=isp3008&lang=eng)
- Application for the Renewal of GIS, Allowance or Allowance for the Survivor (http://www.servicecanada.gc.ca/fi-if/index.jsp?app=prfl&frm=isp3026&lang=eng)

4.5.2 Application for CPP Survivor Benefits

- Application for CPP Survivors' Benefits Online (http://www.servicecanada.gc.ca/eng/online/mysca.shtml)
- Application for CPP Survivors' Benefits By Mail (ISP1200) (http://www.servicecana-

da.gc.ca/fi-if/index.jsp?app=srch&lang=eng#rslt)

- <u>Application for CPP Survivor's and Children's Benefits (ISP1300)</u> (http://www.servicecanada.gc.ca/fi-if/index.jsp?app=prfl&frm=isp1300&lang=eng)

For full-time students between the ages of 18 and 25, you must complete these forms:

- <u>Application for a CPP Child's Benefit (ISP1400)</u> (http://www.servicecanada.gc.ca/fi-if/index.jsp?app=prfl&frm=isp1400&lang=eng)

- <u>Declaration of Attendance at School or University (ISP1401)</u> (http://www.servicecanada.gc.ca/fi-if/index.jsp?app=prfl&frm=isp1401&lang=eng)

4.5.3 Application For QPP Survivors' Benefits

- <u>Application for QPP Survivors' Benefits Online</u> (http://www.rrq.gouv.qc.ca/en/services/services_en_ligne/regime_rentes_quebec/Pages/prestations_survivants.aspx)

- <u>Application for QPP Survivors' Benefits By Mail</u> (https://www.rrq.gouv.qc.ca/SiteCollectionDocuments/www.rrq.gouv.qc/Anglais/formulaires/regime_rentes/deces/B042_en.pdf)

4.5.4 Veteran Affairs Canada

- Application for War Veterans Survivor Benefits (http://www.veterans.gc.ca/eng/forms/document/338)

Chapter 5

When You Have Lived Abroad

Eligibility for public pension benefits in Canada and in most other countries generally requires that you meet some minimum residence or contribution requirements. For example:

- To be eligible for an OAS pension, you must have lived in Canada for at least 10 years after attaining age 18.

- To be eligible to receive your OAS pension (permanently) outside of Canada, you must have lived in Canada for at least 20 years after attaining age 18.

- To be eligible for CPP/QPP disability, death or survivor benefits, you must have contributed for a minimum period.

Meeting these minimum requirements is generally easy if you've lived your entire life in Canada. It is much more difficult if you have moved from or to another country part way through life because you might not qualify for benefits from one or both countries. To resolve complications created by people moving back and forth between countries, Canada has negotiated over 55 social security agreements to coordinate the social security programs between Canada and other countries.

5.1 Social Security Agreement

If you do not meet the eligibility requirements for an OAS pension, you may qualify for a partial pension under an international social security agreement if you have resided in Canada for one full year prior to the application. A social security agreement is an international agreement between two countries designed to coordinate the social security programs of the two countries for people who have worked or lived in both countries. Canada has signed social security agreements with 55 countries. The requirements under the social security agreements vary from agreement to agreement. Please check the details of the agreement that relates to you.

Countries That Have Social Security Agreements with Canada			
Antigua and Barbuda	Austria	Barbados	Belgium
Brazil	Bulgaria	Chile	Croatia
Cyprus	Czech Republic	Denmark	Dominica
Estonia	Finland	France	Germany
Greece	Grenada	Guernsey	Hungary
Iceland	Ireland	Israel	Italy
Jamaica	Japan	Jersey	Korea
Latvia	Lithuania	Luxembourg	Macedonia
Malta	Mexico	Morocco	Netherlands
Norway	Philippines	Poland	Portugal
Romania	Saint Lucia	Saint Vincent and the Grenadines	Serbia
Slovak Republic	Slovenia	Spain	St. Kitts-Nevis
Sweden	Switzerland	Trinidad and	Turkey

Countries That Have Social Security Agreements with Canada		
United Kingdom	Tobago United States	Uruguay

Source: Canada Revenue Agency

5.2 How Can a Social Security Agreement Help Me Qualify for Benefits?

A social security agreement can help you qualify for benefits by allowing you to combine your periods of contribution or residence in Canada and other countries to meet the minimum eligibility requirements.

Although social security agreements can help you meet the minimum contributory or residency requirements to receive benefits, they don't affect those benefits.

For example, Eduardo immigrated to Canada from Spain when he was 60 years old. Without a social security agreement, he wouldn't be able to qualify for an OAS pension at age 65 because he would have lived in Canada for less than 10 years. However, because of the social security agreement between Canada and Spain, he can use his period of residence in Spain to help him meet the 10-year requirement for a partial OAS pension. But his partial pension will be calculated based solely on his period of residence in Canada. Here, he will be getting a pro-rated pension equal to one-eighth (5 divided by 40) of the maximum pension.

Likewise, social security agreements may help people to qualify for disability, survivor's and death benefits under the CPP/QPP as each benefit has minimum eligibility requirements. An agreement may allow periods of contribution to the other country's social security system to be added to periods of contribution to the CPP/QPP to meet these conditions. Once eligibility has been established, the benefits are based on the actual contribution to the CPP/QPP.

5.3 Getting Government Benefit Payments Overseas

5.3.1 OAS Pension

The payment of your OAS pension will stop if you leave Canada for over 6 consecutive months unless you:

- Have lived in Canada for at least 20 years after attaining age 18; or
- Have lived and worked in a country with a social security agreement with Canada, and you will meet the 20-year residence requirement under that agreement.

Your pension payment will resume once you return to Canada.

5.3.2 Guaranteed Income Supplement, Allowance, and Allowance for the Survivor

These benefits may be paid outside Canada for only six months following the month of departure from Canada, regardless of how long the person lived in Canada.

5.3.3 Canada/Quebec Pension Plan

CPP/QPP payments are paid anywhere in the world.

5.3.4 Provincial Social Security Supplement Programs

The provincial social security supplements are designed for low-income seniors residing in that province. Your payment will stop after you ceased to be a resident of that province.

5.3.5 Veterans Affairs Canada Program

You must live in Canada to receive the War Veterans Allowance. Veterans in receipt of disability benefits are eligible to receive payments and other pension-related treatment benefits outside of Canada.

5.4 Key Points

- A social security agreement helps people who have moved back and forth among countries to qualify for social security benefits in one or both countries by coordinating the social security program among these countries.
- A social security agreement may help you qualify for benefits, but it will not affect those benefits.
- You must reside in Canada for at least 20 years before you can receive OAS Pension permanently outside of Canada.
- GIS, allowance, and allowance for the survivor benefits may be paid outside Canada for only six months following the month of departure from Canada, regardless of how long you have lived in Canada.
- CPP/QPP benefits and the Veterans' disability benefits are paid anywhere in the world.
- Provincial income supplements are paid only to residents of the province.

5.5 Resources

- Lived or living outside Canada - Pension and benefits - Apply (https://www.canada.ca/

en/services/benefits/publicpensions/cpp/
cpp-international/apply.html)

- [Lived or living outside Canada - Pensions and benefits - How much could you receive](https://www.canada.ca/en/services/benefits/publicpensions/cpp/cpp-international/benefit-amount.html)

Chapter 6

The Government Taketh Away

The taxation of income from Canadian government pensions will depend on whether you are a resident or non-resident for tax.

6.1 Income Tax

If you are a Canadian resident for tax, these benefits are subject to federal and provincial income taxes:

- OAS pension
- CPP/QPP pension, disability, survivor and death benefits
- War Veterans Allowance

These benefits are exempt from federal and provincial income tax:

- Guaranteed income supplement
- Allowance
- Provincial income supplements
- Veteran Affairs disability pension

6.2 Non-Resident Withholding Tax

If you are a non-resident of Canada, you must pay a non-resident withholding tax on your income from government pensions. The standard non-resident withholding tax rate is 25%. However, Canada has tax treaties with some countries that reduce the non-resident tax withheld. This table shows the tax rate that applies to your country of residence.

Canada Withholding Tax Rates for Non-Residents			
Country of Residence	OAS Benefits	CPP/QPP Pensions	CPP/QPP Death Benefits
Argentina	15%	15%	25%
Australia	15%	15%	15%
Azerbaijan	15%	15%	25%
Bangladesh	15%	15%	25%
Barbados	15%	15%	25%
Brazil non-nationals	25%	25%	25%
Brazil nationals	0%	0%	0%
Bulgaria	15%	15%	25%
Colombia	15%	15%	25%
Cyprus	15%	15%	25%
Dominican Republic	18%	18%	25%

| Canada Withholding Tax Rates for Non-Residents ||||
Country of Residence	OAS Benefits	CPP/QPP Pensions	CPP/QPP Death Benefits
Ecuador	15%	15%	25%
Finland	20%	20%	25%
Germany	15%	15%	25%
Greece	15%	15%	25%
Hungary	15%	15%	25%
Ireland	15%	15%	25%
Israel	15%	15%	25%
Italy	25%	15%	25%
Ivory Coast	15%	15%	25%
Kenya	15%	15%	25%
Malaysia	15%	15%	25%
Malta	15%	15%	25%
Mexico	15%	15%	25%
Netherlands	25%	15%	25%
New Zealand	15%	15%	15%
Norway	15%	15%	25%

Canada Withholding Tax Rates for Non-Residents			
Country of Residence	OAS Benefits	CPP/QPP Pensions	CPP/QPP Death Benefits
Papua-New Guinea	15%	15%	25%
Peru	15%	15%	25%
Philippines	25%	25%	25%
Poland	15%	15%	25%
Portugal	15%	15%	25%
Romania	15%	15%	25%
Senegal	15%	15%	25%
Serbia	15%	15%	25%
Spain	15%	15%	25%
Sri Lanka	15%	15%	25%
Switzerland	15%	15%	25%
Tanzania	15%	15%	25%
Trinidad & Tobago	15%	15%	25%
Turkey	15%	15%	25%
United Kingdom	0%	0%	25%

Canada Withholding Tax Rates for Non-Residents			
Country of Residence	OAS Benefits	CPP/QPP Pensions	CPP/QPP Death Benefits
United States	0%	0%	0%
Zambia	15%	15%	25%
Zimbabwe	15%	15%	25%
All other countries	25%	25%	25%

Note that residents of the U.S., U.K., and Nationals of Brazil are exempt from non-resident withholding taxes on OAS and CPP/QPP pension benefits.

6.3 OAS Recovery Tax

The OAS Recovery Tax is a special tax on your OAS pension. It is also known as the OAS clawback. It was instituted in 1989 to reduce the pension payable to those whose annual income exceeds a certain threshold. Your annual income is defined as your net income before adjustments as reported on Line 234 of the federal Income Tax Return. The recovery tax rate is 15%, so you must pay back the government 15% of your annual income exceeding the threshold until the entire OAS pension is eliminated.

Example

In 2015, the OAS clawback threshold was $72,809 (including the OAS pension). For an OAS recipient receiving the maximum pension amount of $563.74 per month, here are the clawback amounts at different income levels:

OAS Clawback Amounts		
2015 Annual Income	2015 Clawback (Annual)	Annual OAS
72,809	0.00	6,764.88
74,500	253.65	6,511.23
79,000	928.65	5,836.23
83,500	1,603.65	5,161.23
88,000	2,278.65	4,486.23
92,500	2,953.65	3,811.23
97,000	3,628.65	3,136.23
101,500	4,303.65	2,461.23
106,000	4,978.65	1,786.23
110,500	5,653.65	1,111.23
117,909	6,764.88	0.00

You can also use the OAS CLAW-BACK Calculator (see the Resource section) to estimate your OAS clawback tax.

You don't know your actual annual income until after the end of the year. Service Canada will withhold an estimate of the clawback at source based on your previous year's tax returns. The actual clawback will be calculated when you file your tax return for the year. This tax will be compared to the clawback withheld. Any excess withheld will be refunded to you. Conversely, if there is a shortfall, you must pay the additional taxes.

If you believe that Service Canada is withholding too much tax on your OAS payment, you can file a request to reduce the old age security recovery tax at source (see Resource section).

6.4 Non-Residents

Because of the terms of the tax treaty between Canada and each country listed below, non-resident seniors living in these countries are exempt from the recovery tax unless they plan to move to a country that is not listed. So, if you are living in one, you only need to pay the non-resident withholding taxes to Canada, that is beside the income tax you must pay in your country of residence.

Canadian Tax Treaty Countries		
Argentina	Australia	Azerbaijan
Bangladesh	Barbados	Bulgaria
Colombia	Cyprus	Dominican Republic
Ecuador	Finland	Germany
Greece	Hungary	Ireland
Israel	Ivory Coast	Kenya
Malaysia	Malta	Mexico
New Zealand	Norway	Papua
New Guinea	Peru	Poland
Portugal	Romania	Senegal
Spain	Sri Lanka	Switzerland
Tanzania	Trinidad and Tobago	Turkey
United Kingdom	United States	Zambia
Zimbabwe		

If you are a non-resident receiving an OAS pension, and if you are not living in one of the above countries, you must file an Old Age Security Return of Income (T1136) to determine if you must pay the recovery tax on your OAS pension based on net world income.

6.5 Clawback on the GIS and the Allowance

The GIS, the Allowance, and Allowance for the Survivor benefits are designed for OAS recipients with little or no income. In the past, the GIS and the allowance clawback were equal to 50% of your income which is your net income before adjustments (Line 234) excluding income from your OAS pension, GIS and allowance benefits. However, with the GIS top-up introduced in 2011, the total clawback rose to 75% for some income brackets. To help seniors determine their GIS and Allowance payment amounts, Service Canada provides a set of tables showing the different maximum allowed income levels for the GIS and Allowance benefits depending on your marital status and whether your spouse is receiving the OAS pension or the Allowance.

- **Table 1** – Single, widowed or divorced OAS recipient
- **Table 2** – Couple, both receiving OAS pensions
- **Table 3** – Couple, OAS recipient with spouse not receiving OAS benefits
- **Table 4** – Couple, OAS recipient with spouse receiving Allowance
- **Table 5** – Single, surviving spouse age 60-64.

These tables apply only to seniors receiving the maximum amounts. Starting with your yearly income excluding income from OAS pensions, GIS, and Allowance, you can look up your monthly GIS or allowance. Here is an abridged version of the tables at different income levels. The amounts are effective April - June 2015.

Table 1: Single, Widowed or Divorced OAS Recipient		
2014 Annual Income	2015/16 Monthly Clawback	Monthly GIS
0	0.00	764.40
3,000	145.83	619.40
6,000	291.67	461.59
9,000	437.50	336.59
12,000	583.33	211.59
15,000	764.40	86.59
17,088	764.40	0.00

Source: Service Canada

Table 2: Couple, Both Receiving OAS Pensions		
2014 Combined Income	2015/16 Monthly Clawback (each)	Monthly GIS (each)
0	0	506.86
3000	62	444.86
6000	145	361.86
9000	223.97	282.89
12000	286.97	219.89
15000	348.97	157.89
18000	411.97	94.89
21000	473.97	32.89
22560	506.86	0

Source: Service Canada

Table 3: Couple, OAS Recipient with Spouse Not Receiving OAS Benefits		
2014 Combined Income	2015/16 Monthly Clawback (each)	Monthly GIS
0	0.00	764.40
4,000	0.00	764.40
8,000	66.00	698.40
12,000	161.81	602.59
16,000	244.81	519.59
20,000	327.81	436.59
24,000	411.81	352.59
28,000	494.81	269.59
32,000	577.81	186.59
36,000	661.81	102.59
40,000	744.81	19.59
40,944	0.00	0.00

Source: Service Canada

Table 4: Couple, OAS Recipient with Spouse Receiving Allowance				
2014 Combined Income	2015/16 Monthly Clawback (GIS)	Monthly Clawback (Allowance)	Monthly GIS	Monthly Allowance
0	0.00	0.00	506.86	1,070.60
3,000	0.00	186.00	506.86	884.60
6,000	20.00	395.00	486.86	675.60
9,000	36.97	597.97	469.89	472.63
12,000	98.97	662.71	407.89	407.89
15,000	160.97	724.71	345.89	345.89
18,000	223.97	787.71	282.89	282.89
21,000	285.97	849.71	220.89	220.89
24,000	312.16	912.71	194.70	157.89
27,000	312.16	974.71	194.70	95.89
30,000	312.16	1,037.71	194.70	32.89
31,584	506.86	1,070.60	0.00	0.00

Source: Service Canada

Table 5: Single, Surviving Spouse Age 60-64

2014 Annual Income	2015/16 Monthly Clawback	Monthly Allowance for the Survivor
0.00	0.00	1,198.58
3,000.00	206.00	992.58
6,000.00	427.81	770.77
9,000.00	613.81	584.77
12,000.00	740.55	458.03
15,000.00	865.55	333.03
18,000.00	990.55	208.03
21,000.00	1,115.55	83.03
23,016.00	1,198.58	0.00

Source: Service Canada

6.6 Key Points

6.6.1 If you are a Canadian Resident:

- CPP/QPP benefits, OAS pension, and War Veterans Allowance are subject to federal and provincial income tax.
- GIS, Allowance, Allowance for the Survivor, Provincial Income Supplements, and VA disability pensions are tax exempt.
- Your OAS pension is subject to clawback if your annual income is above a certain level.
- The recovery tax rate on the OAS pension is 15% of your income above the threshold.
- The clawback rate on the GIS and the Allowances is 50% on income (excluding OAS benefits). However, due to the

- recent change in top-up benefits for the GIS and the allowances, the clawback rate is as high as 75% in some income brackets.
- ❏ You can determine the amount of your GIS and your Allowance clawback by the tables published by Service Canada.

6.6.2 If you are a Non-Resident:

- ❏ You must pay a non-resident withholding tax on your public pension benefits. The standard non-resident tax rate is 25%, but some countries have a lower tax rate due to their tax treaty with Canada.
- ❏ If you are a resident on the list of countries with a tax treaty with Canada, you are exempt from the OAS recovery tax. If you don't live in one, you must file a tax return to calculate and pay the OAS recovery tax based on your worldwide income.

6.7 Resources

- ❏ Canada Revenue Agency (http://www.cra-arc.gc.ca/)
- ❏ Old Age Security Return of Income form (T1136) (http://www.cra-arc.gc.ca/E/pbg/tf/t1136/README.html)
- ❏ OAS CLAW-BACK Calculator (https://www.retirementadvisor.ca/retadv/apps/clawback/clawback.jsp?toolsSubMenu=post)
- ❏ Request to Reduce Old Age Security Recovery Tax at Source (http://www.cra-arc.gc.ca/E/pbg/tf/t1213/README.html)

- Old Age Security payment amounts (http://www.servicecanada.gc.ca/eng/services/pensions/oas/payments/index.shtml)

Part Two

Know Your Employer Pensions and Personal Savings

Chapter 7

Employer Pension Plans

You are among the fortunate ones if you are a member of an employer-sponsored pension plan. If you or your spouse have no employer pension benefits, you may wish to skip this chapter.

A registered pension plan (RPP) is an arrangement by an employer to provide pensions to retired employees in periodic payments. The Income Tax Act provides deductions regarding both employee and employer contributions. There are basically two main types of employer pension plans:

- ❑ Defined benefit pension plan
- ❑ Defined contribution pension plan

7.1 Defined Benefit Pension Plan

With a defined benefit pension plan, your pension is primarily defined by a set formula often based on your career earnings and years of service. A typical formula for calculating a pension in a plan based on the 5-year final average salary would be like this:

Annual pension income = (2% x years of service) x (average of the last five years of income)

If you have been with an employer for 30 years and tyour average income of over the last five years is $80,000, then your pension entitlement would be like this:

$$(2\% \times 30) \times \$80,000 = 60\% \times \$80,000 = \$48,000$$

Once you are vested in a DB plan, you may receive the benefits you accrue while you are a member. If you leave the company before your retirement date, you'll usually be offered a deferred pension or a lump-sum buyout.

With a defined benefit plan, companies are required by law to contribute to the plan based on actuarial calculations of what contributions are needed to fund current and future pension liabilities. Your contributions are pooled into a retirement fund and managed by your employer or pension plan administrator.

7.2 Defined Contribution Pension Plan

With a defined contribution plan, the employees do not know in advance what their pension will be when they retire. The employer's contributions are usually defined based on a set percentage of the employee's salary. Often the employee can also contribute, with the employer matching the contribution up to a certain limit. Increase your contributions to that limit so you can receive the matched contributions from the employer.

The pension funds are invested in individual accounts for each employee. The employee usually has a choice of investments. Know your investment options and decide on an asset allocation you want to hold in your plan.

With defined contribution pension plans, the risk to the employee is that the investments may perform poorly. However, the upside is that if the investments perform well, all profit increases go to the employee. If the company becomes insolvent the employee will lose none of the pension because the funds are in the employee's name.

7.3 Converting to Income

If you have a defined contribution pension plan, or if you have commuted your defined benefit plan into a lump-sum amount, there are two ways for you to commence income from your pension plan proceeds.

7.3.1 Use the plan proceeds to buy a life annuity

You can only buy a life annuity from a life insurance company. Life annuity is a stream of guaranteed future payments for as long as you live. Once a life annuity is set up, it is set for life. At the time of setting up the annuity, there are many options you must consider. These options can have a dramatic effect on income

Single life or joint life
The single life annuity is based on one life. If that person passes away, the annuity payment ends. A joint life annuity is different in that the payment of the annuity is based on two lives instead of one. If one annuitant passes away, then the annuity payment will continue to the surviving annuitant. The annuity payment ends only on the death of the last annuitant. For a joint annuity, you can also decide whether to have the income reduced on the death of the first annuitant.

Guaranteed Period
You can buy a life annuity with guaranteed payments for a minimum number of years such as 10 or 20 years, so the payment will not stop when the annuitant dies before the end of the guaranteed period.

Indexed
For all life annuities, you have an option to increase your income every year by a certain factor. This is typically done to account for increases in the cost of living. However, some insurance companies

may not offer this option; and if they do, it may be offered at a high price.

7.3.2 Move your funds into a Life Income Fund (LIF) or a Locked-in Retirement Income Funds (LRIFs)

These vehicles are subject to minimum withdrawals similar to RRIFs, but unlike RRIFs, they are also subject to maximum annual withdrawals. In some provinces, the LIF or LRIF must be converted to a life annuity at a certain age (usually 80). This option will give you more flexibility than a life annuity but does not protect the risk of outliving the money.

7.4 Key Points

- ❏ There are two employer pension plans—defined benefit plans and defined contribution plans.
- ❏ There are two ways to commence income from your pension plan— (1) Use the funds to purchase an annuity, and (2) Transfer the funds to a LIF or a LRIF.
- ❏ LIF and LRIF are subject to minimum and maximum annual withdrawals.

Chapter 8

Your Personal Tax Shelter

This chapter will summarize the common tax-shelters available to individuals under the *Income Tax Act*.

8.1 Registered Retirement Savings Plan

A *Registered Retirement Savings Plan* (RRSP) is a contract between an individual and a financial institution, which is registered under the *Income Tax Act*. The individual contributing funds to the plan, within certain parameters established by the Act, receives a tax deduction for his contributions, and draws a taxable income from the plan at retirement. An individual who has earned income can contribute to a plan in their own name, up to the end of the year when they turn 71. An individual past this age who still has earned income can contribute to the plan of a younger spouse, up to the end of the end the spouse turns 71.

An RRSP is your own personal defined contribution pension plan. You know what you are putting into your plan, but you don't know what income you will get when you retire.

The limit for calculating your RRSP contribution room is 18 percent of your previous year's earned income, up to a certain limit. The limit for 2017 is $26,010. If you also belong to an employer pension plan or deferred profit sharing plan, the overall limit will be reduced by the Pension Adjustment, which represents the value of your participation in the employer's plan for the year.

You can open as many RRSPs as you like in any financial institution. You may transfer your funds from one RRSP to another without penalty.

You may withdraw part of your assets from a plan without having the whole plan terminated, but the withdrawals are taxable at your marginal rate and will be counted as income for the OAS recovery tax.

You can contribute to an RRSP until the end of the year when you turn 71. At that point, you must do one of the three things: (1) take the cash (and pay the taxes), (2) buy a life annuity, or (3) transfer the assets to an RRIF (which will be discussed later in the chapter).

If you die with an RRSP portfolio, the plan will be terminated, and the entire proceeds will be taxable at your marginal rate, which will be very high if you have a large portfolio. You may have to pay probate and/or estate taxes depending on your individual situation. To put it differently, it is not a good idea to die with an RRSP. To avoid paying too much tax when you die, you need an RRSP withdrawal strategy to withdraw assets from the plan before you die and while your marginal tax rate is low. You will learn more about the strategy in Section 10.3.

People with high income receive big tax benefits from RRSPs. They get a tax deduction for their contributions at high tax rates, and their investment income accumulates on a tax-deferred basis within the plan. Later, they pay a lower tax rate on their withdrawals since their income usually falls in retirement.

People with low income receive very few tax benefits from RRSPs and yet if they take money out, the withdrawal is counted as income, subject to income tax, and potentially reduce their OAS benefits.

8.2 Spousal RRSP

Spousal RRSP is an RRSP that names the contributor's spouse as the annuitant. The contributor contributes from his or her own contribution room. It can be a vehicle to split income for high-income individuals.

8.3 Registered Retirement Income Funds

A *Registered Retirement Income Fund* (RRIF) is a trust fund registered with the *Income Tax Act*. Usually, an RRIF is set up with funds transferred on a tax-deferred basis from an RRSP. Once the RRIF is opened, annual withdrawals must be made, beginning the following calendar year. Different withdrawal schedules apply, depending on when the RRIF is set up. All RRIF withdrawals are taxable in the year received. If you have a large RRIF portfolio, these minimum withdrawals will increase your marginal tax rate and cause an OAS clawback.

8.4 Tax-Free Savings Accounts

A *Tax-Free Savings Account* (TFSA) allows a Canadian resident over the age of 18 to contribute (up to a certain limit per year) in after-tax money. There is no tax deduction for contributions to a TFSA, but the investment income accumulates tax-free. The funds can be withdrawn at any time, and no tax is payable on either capital or income on withdrawal. There are three features of these plans:

- ❏ Contributions are not based on income.
- ❏ Cumulative used contribution rooms can be carried forward indefinitely
- ❏ Very flexible "in-out" provisions -- any withdrawals restore contribution room

The contribution room for 2009 is $5,000 per person. This contribution limit will be indexed to the CPI every year in increments of $500. For example, for 2009 - 2011, the limit is $5,000; and for 2013 - 2014, the limit is $5,500; and so on.

Remember that TFSAs are not as flexible as regular savings accounts. If you are not careful about how much you contribute and withdraw, you can be charged a penalty by the Canada Revenue Agency.

8.5 Key Points

- An RRSP is your own personal defined contribution pension plan.
- A spousal RRSP can be a vehicle to split income for high-income individuals.
- A TFSA allows you to accumulate investment income on your assets tax-free.

Part Three

Know the Secrets To Maximizing Your Retirement Income from Government Pensions

Chapter 9

Finding Out Where You Stand

In part one of this book, you have learned what the government's public pension system will give and take away from you. In Part Two, you have learned the basics of employer pension plans and your own personal tax-sheltered savings. It is time for us to put it all together, so you can maximize the amount that your government will give to you, and minimize the amount that your government will take away from you.

In planning your retirement, you must consider how you want to live in retirement, how much it will cost, and where your future income comes from. You probably have a good idea about the first two items. It is the last item we need to focus on, and you must know where you stand on the sources of future income.

For most people, there are four main sources of retirement income.

- ❑ Government pensions.
- ❑ Your employer's pension plan.
- ❑ Your RRSPs/RRIFs.
- ❑ Investment income.

The rest of this chapter will provide you with a blueprint to maximize your income from government pensions.

9.1 Don't Miss Out on Your Government Benefits

Public pensions play an important role in your retirement finances and you sure don't want to miss out on it.

- ❏ If you have lived and worked in Canada, you may be eligible for benefits from OAS pension and Canada/Quebec Pension Plan.
- ❏ If you have low income, you may be eligible for GIS, Allowances, and the provincial income supplement programs.
- ❏ If you are a veteran, you may be eligible for benefits from the Veterans Affairs Canada Program.
- ❏ If you have lived abroad, you may be eligible for public pensions of that country.

Many people missed out on government benefits because they didn't know what benefits they are eligible for and how to apply. With the knowledge from Part One of this book, you may be able to claim your entitlements.

9.2 Find Out Where You Stand on Your CPP and QPP

For most people, the CPP/QPP is a big source of their future income. And it is easy to find out where you stand on your contributions to the CPP/QPP.

If you have contributed to the CPP, you can get a statement of Contributions from Service Canada by using the My Service Canada Account online service. You can also get an estimate of your retirement pension now and at the age of 65. You can get the estimates over the phone by calling Service Canada at 1-800-277-9914 and pressing 0 to talk to an agent. You can ask the agent to give you estimates of your pension based on various scenarios such as taking early retirement at age 60 or postponing your retirement until age 70, etc.

If you have contributed to the QPP, you can get access to your QPP Statements of Participation and get estimates on your retirement pension now and at age 65 by using the My Account at the Rǔgie online service.

9.3 Estimate Your Future Income Stream

Before you can formulate a strategy to maximize your total retirement income, you must know your future income stream because it will affect your OAS benefits which are income-tested. You can use the Canadian Retirement Income Calculator to do the projections. See the Resource section for more information on the calculator.

The calculator will help you better understand how each pillar of the retirement income system will contribute to your future income stream. You will need to work through a series of modules to estimate your income from the different sources. To get the most out of your session, you will need this information:

- ❑ CPP Statement of Contributions or QPP Statement of Participation;
- ❑ Financial information about your employer pension (if applicable);
- ❑ Recent RRSP, RRIF statements (if applicable); and
- ❑ Statements of other savings that will provide ongoing monthly income (annuities, foreign pensions, survivor pensions, regular investment accounts, etc.).

9.4 Estimate Your Potential OAS Clawback

Review Section 6.4 regarding clawbacks on GIS and the Allowances and use the five tables from the Service Canada website to determine if you will be eligible for the GIS and the Allowance benefits. See the Resource section for the URL of the website.

If your projected income is low enough for you to qualify for the GIS/Allowance benefits, follow the strategies outlined in section 11.1 to maximize your GIS benefits.

If your projected income is too high for the GIS benefits, check to see if you are subject to OAS clawback. If so, you should follow the strategies outlined in Section 11.2 to minimize your OAS clawback.

9.5 Key Points

- In planning for your retirement, consider all potential sources of retirement income.
- Don't miss out on your public pension benefits.
- Use the Retirement Income Calculator to estimate your future income stream.
- The level of your future income will determine what strategies you should use to maximize your income from public pensions.

9.6 Resources

- Canadian Retirement Income Calculator (http://www.servicecanada.gc.ca/eng/services/pensions/cric.shtml)
- Use the five tables on this page (http://www.servicecanada.gc.ca/eng/services/

pensions/oas/payments/index.shtml) to determine if you are eligible for the GIS and Allowances benefits.

Chapter 10

Maximizing Your Public Pensions

As you went through the steps outlined in the last chapter to estimate your potential retirement income from the various sources, you will notice that the income from most of the sources is predictable except for investment income (especially capital gains) from your personal savings, and withdrawals from your RRSP/RRIFs. With that in mind, let's walk through the strategies you can implement to maximize your public pension and minimize OAS clawback.

10.1 CPP/QPP Claiming Strategies

These strategies increase the overall value of your CPP/QPP retirement pension, with the potential to lower your income taxes and OAS clawbacks.

10.1.1 Determine When to Start Your CPP/QPP Retirement Pension

The standard age to receive your retirement pension is 65. However, you can take a reduced pension as early as age 60 or take an increased pension after age 65. Whatever strategy you want to implement depends entirely on your individual situation. Here are some considerations:

- If you are still working, consider delaying your pension until you retire. In return, you will receive an increased pension, which will be taxed at a lower rate after your retirement.
- If you are ill and have a diminished life expectancy, consider starting your pension early.
- If you are female, healthy, and have a high probability of living beyond the age of 90, consider delaying your CPP/QPP pension.
- Because the payment of the pension stops when you die, there is no estate value other than the $2,500 death benefit and a reduced survivor pension for your spouse. It makes sense to start your pension early and use the income to pay your bills before tapping into your own personal assets. If you don't need it to pay your bills, you can always redirect it to your TFSAs or non-registered accounts. That's how you can build up your estate value. Money in hand is always better than the money you could get only by out-living your life expectancy.

10.1.2 Take advantage of the Child Rearing (CR) Provision

The CR provision is a provision under the CPP for you to exclude from the calculation of your pension the time you spent with no or low earnings while you are caring for a young child. This ensures that reduced earnings during the first 7 years of your child's life will not result in lower pension benefits. To apply for the CR provision, complete a special form when you apply for any CPP benefit. Either parent is eligible.

10.1.3 Pension Sharing with Your Spouse

You can share your CPP/QPP pension with your spouse. By sharing your CPP/QPP pension with your spouse, you have the potential to reduce income tax and OAS clawback.

You can share your CPP with your spouse by making a request to Service Canada (Pension sharing form ISP-1002 Application for Pension Sharing of Retirement Pensions CPP). Once a pension sharing application has been approved, the pensions will be divided at the source and revised amounts sent out to each spouse.

The Quebec Pension Plan also has a provision for pension sharing, but with different eligibility requirements.

10.2 Income Splitting Strategies

Splitting income with your spouse may enable you to lower the income of the higher-earning spouse so you can reduce income tax and OAS clawback.

10.2.1 Pension Splitting

For most people, the most effective way to split pension income (that includes most types of pension, but excludes the OAS and the CPP/QPP pension) is by filing an election with the "Form T1032 Joint Election to Split Pension Income in you and your spouse's income tax return. Here is an example of the effectiveness of pension splitting.

Before Pension Splitting

	Husband	Wife	Total
Pension Income	73,000	0	73,000
Interest Income	40,500	15,000	55,500
CPP	3,500	3,500	7,000
OAS (after clawback)	0	6,765	6,765
Total Income	117,000	25,265	142,265
Tax Payable	33,302	3,106	36,408
After-tax Income	83,698	22,159	105,857

After Pension Splitting

	Husband	Wife	Total
Pension Income	36,500	36,500	73,000
Interest Income	40,500	15,000	55,500
CPP	3,500	3,500	7,000
OAS (after clawback)	5,611	6,765	12,376
Total Income	86,111	61,765	147,876
Tax Payable	20,174	12,231	32,405
After-tax Income	65,937	49,534	115,471

In this example, the husband has elected to split his pension income 50/50 to his wife resulting in an income tax saving of $4,003, and a reduction in OAS clawback from $6,765 to $1,154 for the husband. With this simple strategy, the couple has increased their after-tax income by $9,614.

10.2.2 Pension Sharing With Spouse

This is the same strategy as discussed in Section 10.1(C). It is repeated here for completeness.

10.2.3 Use of Spousal RRSP

If you have a higher income now or expect to have a higher retirement income than your spouse, consider taking advantage of a Spousal RRSP right away. Spousal RRSP is one practical means of income splitting for this situation. They can help defer taxes right away, and reduce taxes in retirement when you take money out of the Spousal RRSP taxed at the (lower) tax rate of your spouse.

10.3 RRSP Withdrawal Strategies

The conventional wisdom regarding retirement income has always been to use up non-registered assets first and defer withdrawing from your RRSPs for as long as possible to maximize tax-deferred growth. Depending on your circumstances, this might not be the best strategy.

10.3.1 Reasons why the deferral of taking RRSP and RRIF into income may not make sense:

- You cannot defer taking your RRSP and RRIF into income indefinitely. By law, you must collapse your entire RRSP portfolio or convert it into an income option by December 31 of the year you turn 71. If you convert your RRSP to an RRIF, which offers the greatest tax deferral opportunity, you will have to take these assets into income, according to the RRIF minimum withdrawal requirements which increase with your age. This additional income could put you in a higher marginal tax bracket and result in higher taxes on the income, and a potential clawback of some or all of your OAS benefits.

- In death, the RRSPs were deemed to have collapsed. Generally, the value of the RRSP/RRIF at the date of death is included in the income of the deceased on the tax return for the year of death. The tax consequences depend on who is listed as the beneficiary of the RRSP. So, you might pay a lot of taxes if you died without a good estate plan.

10.3.2 Here are strategies for you to convert your RRSP funds into non-registered assets with minimal tax impacts:

- ❏ If you have no pension income when you reach age 65, convert a portion of your RRSP to an RRIF to maximize on pension income tax credits. This tax credit is non-refundable and is equal to the lesser of your pension income or $2,000. With this tax credit, you are effectively withdrawing from your RRIF tax-free. So cash out as much from your RRIF as possible to utilize the credit.

- ❏ If you have a small RRSP portfolio, or if you retire early, you can withdraw your entire RRSP well before you turn 65 and deposit the net proceeds (after income taxes) into your TFSA. This results in extra income taxes but reduces future GIS/OAS clawbacks.

- ❏ If you have a large RRSP portfolio, start your RRSP withdrawals when you are in a lower income tax bracket right after you are retired so that when you are 71 you could have reduced your Required Minimum Distribution (RMD) to where it would be under the income threshold for OAS clawback. You can do it in large chunks every other year. For example, if you must withdraw $30,000 annually, you might withdraw $60,000 every other year. This technique might allow you to earn OAS/GIS in alternate years.

- ❏ If at age 71 your RMD is still too large, you can withdraw a larger portion in the next couple of years. You might miss your OAS/GIS pension for those years, but then it would help to manage your OAS/GIS clawback.

10.4 Savings and Investment Strategies

10.4.1 Maximize Your Contributions to TFSAs

Maximize your and your spouse's contribution to TFSAs, especially if your investment income will put you over the OAS recovery tax threshold. Unlike RRSP withdrawals, money taken from a TFSA is not counted as income and is not subject to tax and will not affect your OAS benefits.

10.4.2 Pay off Your Mortgage/Debt

If you own a home, consider using part of your savings to pay off your mortgage. Like contributing to a TFSA, money used to pay off your mortgage will not generate investment income, which is good if you are facing OAS clawback. It also reduces your interest expenses so you will need less income to maintain the same lifestyle.

10.4.3 Seek Tax Efficient Investments for Your Non-Registered Assets

If you have investments in regular investment accounts, consider allocating more assets to tax efficient investments. For example, capital gain is preferable to interest income because only one-half of your capital gain is counted as income while interest income is counted. Dividends are less desirable because they are subject to 38% gross-up which causes your income to be inflated, not a good outcome for OAS planning.

10.4.4 Watch for Capital Dispositions After Age 65

People with significant unrealized capital gains from real properties or investments may be better off triggering those gains before receiving their OAS pensions. Triggering them after may cause th loss of OAS benefits from clawbacks.

If you must realize capital gains after age 65, find out whether you have any unrealized capital losses you can harvest and use it to offset the gains in the same calendar year, so you will be reporting a smaller net amount in your tax return. This is important. A loss carried forward or back will not help to reduce your OAS clawback because your OAS clawback is calculated based on your net income before applying the loss carried forward or back. The only way to offset your gains with your losses in the calculation of the clawback is for the gains and losses to occur in the same calendar year so you net the two together in your tax return.

10.5 Key Points

- When to start your CPP/QPP retirement pensions depends on your own individual situation. However, because the pension does not have estate value when you die, I found it more beneficial to start your pensions early so you can build up your estate value with the pension income.
- Take advantage of the Child Rearing Provision.
- Split income with your spouse.
- Convert RRSPs to a RRIF at age 65 to take advantage of the pension income tax credit if you don't have a pension income.
- Unloading your RRSPs and RRIFs way before age 65. Otherwise unload them in large amounts in a short, concentrated period to minimize long periods of OAS clawback.
- Put all your savings into TFSAs and pay off your mortgage and debt.
- Put non-registered savings in tax-efficient assets.

- Watch out for capital dispositions after age 65.

10.6 Resources

- Application for CPP Child Rearing Provision (ISP1640) (http://www.servicecanada.gc.ca/fi-if/index.jsp?app=prfl&frm=isp1640&lang=eng)

- Application for Pension Sharing of CPP Retirement Pensions (ISP1002) (http://www.servicecanada.gc.ca/fi-if/index.jsp?app=prfl&frm=isp1002&lang=eng)

- Application for QPP Retirement Pension Sharing Between Spouses (http://www.rrq.gouv.qc.ca/SiteCollectionDocuments/www.rrq.gouv.qc/Anglais/formulaires/regime_rentes/Retraite/RRQ060_en.pdf)

- T1032 Joint Election to Split Pension Income (http://www.cra-arc.gc.ca/E/pbg/tf/t1032/)

Chapter 11

Applying to Specific Situations

Now that you have learned the basic strategies for maximizing your government pension income, let's see how you can apply them to two specific situations.

11.1 Individuals With Low Income

If you think your annual income will be low enough to be eligible for the GIS benefits when you reach age 65, apply for the OAS pension early, and then maximize your GIS benefits by minimizing your reported net income. Remember that if you are eligible for the GIS, your spouse may be eligible for the allowance, and you and your spouse may also be eligible for the provincial income supplements.

Depending on your own individual situation, here are some strategies you can implement.

11.1.1 CPP/QPP Claiming Strategies

Start Your CPP/QPP Retirement Pensions Early

When approaching age 60 and thinking that you may qualify for the GIS benefit, your best course of action is to start the CPP/QPP retirement pension benefits early. By taking early retirement, you will be receiving a lower pension, so there will be a smaller GIS clawback. Meanwhile, you have collected a pension earlier and are benefiting from the extra income. However, if you are also receiving social assistance before age 65, taking early retirement is not an attractive option, because the social benefits will simply be reduced dollar for dollar by the pension.

Take advantage of the Child Rearing Provision

The CR provision will increase your CPP/QPP pension if you qualify. See Section 10.1(B) for more information.

Pension Sharing with Spouse

This strategy may help you to reduce your total tax payable, which is always good. However, it does not affect your GIS and Allowance benefits because your GIS/Allowance eligibility depends on your combined income. See section 10.1(C) for more information.

11.1.2 Income Splitting Strategies

Income splitting strategies may help you to reduce your total tax payable, which is always good. However, they do not affect your GIS and Allowance benefits because your GIS/Allowance eligibility depends on your combined income. See section 10.2 for more information.

11.1.3 RRSP Strategies

Use RRSPs to Enhance Your GIS Benefits After 65

As we have seen, contributing to an RRSP before the age of 65 has no real benefit for low-income people. But for people whose incomes are a little over the GIS eligibility limit, or who are eligible for only a partial GIS, contributing to an RRSP after age 65 might make a lot of sense. OAS pension and the GIS begin at age 65. People can keep contributing to RRSPs until they turn 71. Contributing to an RRSP effectively lowers a person's income for GIS eligibility. If a 65-year old with a very modest income has some RRSP contribution room, they can contribute enough money to an RRSP to allow them access to the GIS.

RRSP Withdrawal Strategies

Use RRSP withdrawal strategies (section 10.3) to maximize your GIS benefits by minimizing clawback due to income from RRSP withdrawals.

11.1.4 Savings and Investment Strategies

Shelter your investment income from GIS clawback by TFSAs. Pay off all your debts and seek tax efficient investments for your non-registered assets. See section 10.4 for more information.

11.2 Individuals With High Income

If you think that your net income after retirement might be high enough to trigger an OAS clawback, implement these strategies to minimize the clawback. Minimizing the clawback means reducing your income. Here are some strategies that you could implement.

11.2.1 CPP/QPP Claiming Strategies

When to Start Your CPP/QPP Retirement Pension

Consider delaying your retirement pension to avoid triggering the clawback. In return, you will receive an increased pension.

Take Advantage of the Child Rearing Provision

The CR provision will increase your CPP/QPP pension if you qualify. See Section 10.1(B) for more information.

Pension Sharing with Spouse

Sharing your CPP/QPP income with your spouse may enable you to lower the income of the higher-earning spouse and reduce the total income tax bill and reduce your OAS clawback. See section 10.1(C) for more information.

11.2.2 Income Splitting Strategies

Splitting income with your spouse may enable you to lower the income of the higher-earning spouse and reduce the total income tax bill and reduce your OAS clawback. See section 10.2 for more information.

11.2.3 RRSP Withdrawal Strategies

Use the RRSP withdrawal strategies as discussed in section 10.3 to minimize your OAS clawback due to income from RRSP withdrawals. See section 10.3 for more information.

11.2.4 Savings and Investment Strategies

Shelter your investment income from the OAS clawback by TFSAs. Pay off all your debts and seek tax efficient investments for your non-registered assets. See section 10.4 for more information.

11.3 Key Points

11.3.1 If you are a low-income earner:

- ❏ Your retirement income strategy should be focused on maximizing the GIS benefits.
- ❏ Take early retirements from CPP/QPP to receive a lower payment (hence less GIS clawback) for longer periods.
- ❏ Other strategies described in Chapter 10 apply here.

11.3.2 If you are a high-income earner:

❏ Your retirement income should be focused on minimizing OAS clawbacks.

❏ Delay your CPP/QPP pension to minimize the OAS clawback and maximize future payout amounts.

❏ Other strategies described in Chapter 10 apply here.

Chapter 12

The Grass Is Greener

"WHEN CANADIANS THINK of tax havens, they rarely think of the U.S., but it truly is one of the best options available for Canadians today," according to Robert Keats, an internationally renowned expert in cross-border financial planning and author of the book "*A Canadian's Best Tax Haven: The US.*"

If you are eligible for an OAS pension and have lived in Canada for over 20 years, you could maximize income from your Canadian public pensions after-tax by leaving Canada and emigrating to the U.S. Here are the tax benefits for Canadian Non-residents residing in the U.S. receiving Canadian public pensions.

12.1 Non-Resident Withholding Tax

Because of the tax treaty between the U.S. and Canada, the income from Canadian public pensions payable to U.S. residents is exempt from non-resident withholding taxes.

12.2 Income Tax

When you file tax returns in the U.S. as a resident, the income from Canadian public pensions is taxed in a manner like U.S. Social Security benefits. That means married couples with incomes of less than US$32,000 (including the Canadian public pension income) or a single person with less than US$25,000 of income pays no U.S. tax on this income. The income from Canadian public pensions is free from both Canadian and U.S. taxes for people in this income bracket. For those at the higher income levels, only 85% of the Canadian public pension income is taxed at the standard U.S. tax rate; the other 15% is tax-free.

12.3 OAS Recovery Tax

Canadians are exampt from the OAS recovery tax once they become U.S. residents. For a high-income married couple, this could mean an immediate tax saving on their OAS pension alone of up to CAD $13,500, depending on which U.S. tax bracket they fall into. Even Canadians with sufficient income to put them in the highest U.S. bracket with surplus foreign tax credits from other sources, such as RRSP withdrawals, may use these foreign tax credits to zero out any U.S. taxes due so they pay zero percent net on their OAS pension income that normally would have been at 100% net tax had they remained Canadian residents.

Example: couple with CPP: 11,000 and OAS: 6,750 subject to 100% clawback. Canadian tax bracket (Ontario: 46.4%). U.S. tax bracket (Florida: 25%).

Tax Savings on Public Pension Benefits		
	Canadian Resident	US Resident
OAS Pension	11,000	9,350
CPP Pension	6,750	5,738
Taxable Income	17,750	15,088
OAS Recovery Tax	6,750	0
Marginal Income Tax Rate	46.4%	25.0%
Income tax	5,104	3,772
Tax Due	11,854	3,772
Effective Tax Rate	67%	21%
Total Savings		8,082

12.4 Registered Retirement Savings Plans

Without proper planning, RRSPs can create unnecessary U.S. taxes and can be double-taxed or overtaxed by the U.S. and Canada. But they can be a great source of tax savings if you plan for them correctly. An optimized solution is to remove your RRSPs out of Canada with as close to zero net tax as possible. However, this is a strategy that you should not attempt to implement on your own. I recommend that you use an experienced cross-border financial planner trained in all aspects of Canadian and U.S. investments and taxes to guide you in the right direction.

12.5 Complications

But retiring and living in the US might not be for everyone. Here are some issues and implications:

❏ **Healthcare** – as a non-resident of Canada, you will not be covered by Canada's publicly funded health care system.

- **U.S. Estate Taxes** – as a U.S. resident, you are subject to U.S. estate taxes on your worldwide assets. The maximum tax rate in 2014 is 40%.

- **Giving Up Canadian Residency** – To be deemed a non-resident of Canada, you must sever your ties with Canada. That means you must sell your principal residence, close all your bank and investment accounts, and plan not to return to Canada for at least two years after leaving, etc.

- **Departure tax** – When you become a non-resident of Canada, you must file an exit return and pay taxes on the income for the year, plus the capital gains on the deemed disposition of certain assets.

Also, you might not want to be far away from your immediate family when you are getting older. So, do not decide to emigrate to the U.S. based solely on taxes.

12.6 Key Points

- Under the U.S.-Canada tax treaty, Canadian public pension benefits paid to U.S. residents are exempt from non-resident withholding taxes.

- Canadian public pension benefits paid to U.S. residents are taxed at a lower U.S. tax rate compared to Canadian residents

- U.S. residents are exempt from the OAS recovery tax.

- You can achieve great tax savings with your RRSPs, but recommend the use of a professional cross-border financial planner.

- There are other issues to consider before you implement this strategy.

Conclusion

TO SUMMARIZE, CANADA'S public pension system is an important source of retirement income for most Canadians. If you are nearing retirement or in retirement, understand how these government benefits play a role in your retirement income.

To get the most benefit from the book, focus on the eligibility requirements for the public pensions, especially on spousal and family benefits as they are usually missed out by people. Don't just assume you won't qualify. Even the rich can qualify for the Guaranteed Income Supplement if they have a low income after retirement. Remember, the GIS benefit is based on income, not wealth.

Knowing where you stand is the first and most necessary step in effective retirement planning. You can obtain your CPP/QPP contribution history and estimated amount of pension from the government. With the Canadian Retirement Income Calculator, you can estimate your future income stream from the various sources of retirement income. This information will help you formulate an optimal strategy to maximize your income from public pensions.

Take the time to understand the strategies described in chapter 10 to maximize your public pension income. When implemented correctly, these strategies can reduce your taxes and the OAS and GIS clawback.

All the theory in the world is useless unless you can apply it to yourself. Remember, you must act. Engage the services of a financial professional if you must.

I hope this book has served its purpose to increase your knowledge, skill, and confidence to make responsible financial decisions regarding your retirement planning.

You've made it through the book, great job! But remember, true knowledge is applied knowledge. It may apply to you, or to someone you know, like your family members or friends near retirement. If you found this book useful, I'd appreciate if you could write a review of this book to let others know about the benefits you've got from it. This will not only help others to maximize their retirement income from public pensions, but it is rewarding for me to know how much work has benefited others.

Thank you!

Exhibit I

Government Benefits Administration Offices

Service Canada Offices

Toll-Free:1-800-277-9914 TTY:1-800-255-4786
Callers outside Canada and the United States can call collect: 613-957-1954,
Monday to Friday from 8:30 a.m. to 4:30 p.m. Eastern Time
Website: http://www.servicecanada.gc.ca
My Service Canada Account sign-in page (http://www.service-canada.gc.ca/eng/online/mysca.shtml)
Service Canada Online Services and Forms (http://www.servoce-camada.gc.ca/eng/online/index.shtml)

Regional Offices:

Newfoundland and Labrador
Service Canada
PO Box 9430 Station A
St. John's NL A1A 2Y5

Prince Edward Island
Service Canada
PO Box 8000 Station Central
Charlottetown PE C1A 8K1

Nova Scotia
Service Canada
PO Box 1687 Station Central
Halifax NS B3J 3J4

New Brunswick
Service Canada
PO Box 250 Station A
Fredericton NB E3B 4Z6

Quebec
For Old Age Security Program related requests
Service Canada
PO Box 1816 Station Terminus
Quebec QC G1K 7L5

For Canada Pension Plan related requests
Service Canada
PO Box 250 Station A
Fredericton NB E3B 4Z6

Ontario

For postal codes beginning with L or M
Service Canada
PO Box 5100 Station D
Scarborough ON M1R 5C8

For postal codes beginning with K or P
Service Canada
PO Box 2013
Timmins ON P4N 8C8

For postal codes beginning with N
Service Canada
PO Box 2020 Station Main
Chatham ON N7M 6B2

Quebec Pension Plan Portal

Quĭbec Pension Plan (QPP)
Rŭgie des rentes du Quĭbec

Case postale 5200
Quйbec (Quйbec) G1K 7S9
Quebec region: 418-643-5185
Montreal region: 514-873-2433
Toll-free: 1-800-463-5185
Monday to Friday 8:00 a.m. to 5:00 p.m
Website: http://www.rrq.gouv.qc.ca/
My Account at the Rйgie Sign-in Page (http://www.rrq.gouv.qc.ca/en/services/services_en_ligne/mon_dossier_regie/Pages/mon_dossier_regie.aspx)

Veterans Affairs Canada

Veterans Affairs Canada
PO Box 6000
Matane, QC
G4W 0E4
Phone: 1-866-522-2122 (toll-free)
Monday to Friday, 8:30 to 4:30, local time.
Email: information@vac-acc.gc.ca
Website: http://www.veterans.gc.ca/

Exhibit II

Provincial Income Supplement Programs

- British Columbia: Seniors Supplement (http://www2.gov.bc.ca/gov/content/governments/policies-for-government/bcea-policy-and-procedure-manual/general-supplements-and-programs/seniors-supplement)

- Alberta: Seniors Benefit Program (http://www.seniors.alberta.ca/seniors/seniors-benefit-program.html)

- Saskatchewan: Assistance Program (http://www.saskatchewan.ca/residents/family-and-social-support/seniors-services/financial-help-for-seniors#benefits)

- Manitoba: 55 Plus (http://www.gov.mb.ca/fs/eia/55plus.html)

- Ontario: G.A.I.N.S. (Guaranteed Annual Income System) (http://www.fin.gov.on.ca/en/credit/gains/)

- New Brunswick: Low Income Seniors Benefit (http://www2.gnb.ca/content/gnb/en/departments/finance/promo/seniors.html)

- Nova Scotia - Seniors Provincial Income Tax Refund (http://www.novascotia.ca/finance/en/home/taxation/tax101/personal-incometax/GISrefundFAQ.aspx)

- [Newfoundland and Labrador: Low Income Seniors Benefit](http://www.fin.gov.nl.ca/fin/tax_programs_incentives/personal/income_supplement.html)
- [Yukon: Low Income Seniors' Supplement](http://www.hss.gov.yk.ca/ysis.php)
- [Northwest Territories: Senior Citizens Supplementary Benefit](http://www.hss.gov.nt.ca/sites/www.hss.gov.nt.ca/files/seniors-program-extended-health-benefits.pdf)
- [Nunavut: Senior Citizens Supplementary Benefit](http://gov.nu.ca/family-services/information/senior-citizen-supplementary-benefit-scsb)
- [Quebec](http://www.msss.gouv.qc.ca/en/sujets/groupes/seniors.php)
- [Prince Edward Island: Supports for Seniors](http://www.gov.pe.ca/seniors/)

Exhibit III

Documents Required by the OAS Application

Proof of date of birth

You don't need to provide proof of the date of birth with your application. However, Service Canada may request proof of the date of birth.

Proof of Canadian Legal Status

If you were born in Canada and have lived in Canada all your life, you need not prove your legal status.

If you were born in Canada and became a citizen of another country before February 15, 1977, you may have given up your Canadian citizenship. If you are not sure about your status, you can contact a Canadian Citizenship and Immigration office.

If you were born outside of Canada, a certified photocopy of one of these documents is required:

- Canadian citizens: certificate of Canadian citizenship, naturalization certificate, or Canadian passport issued in 1970 or later;
- Permanent residents: Canadian immigration documents or Canadian immigration stamps on your passport;
- A resident under a temporary resident's permit: temporary resident's permit.

Proof of Residence History

If you have not lived in Canada all your life, you must provide certified photocopies of documents to prove when you entered, departed or returned to Canada. Examples of such documents are:

- ❏ Passports
- ❏ Immigration records
- ❏ Customs declarations

If you no longer have your original immigration documents. Service Canada may obtain information from Citizenship and Immigration Canada on your behalf. For Service Canada to obtain this information, you must complete, sign and return the Consent to Exchange information with Citizenship and Immigration Canada (ISP3210) (http://www.servicecanada.gc.ca/fi-if/index.jsp?app=prfl&frm=isp3210&lang=eng) with your OAS application.

Acronyms

CPI	Consumer Price Index
CPP	Canada Pension Plan
CPP/QPP	Canada/Quebec Pension Plans
EPP	Employer Pension Plan
GIS	Guaranteed Income Supplement
LIF	Life Income Fund
LRIF	Locked-in Retirement Income Fund
MSCA	My Service Canada Account
OAS	Old Age Security
PRB	Post-Retirement Benefits (CPP)
QPP	Quebec Pension Plan
RMD	Required Minimum Distribution
RPP	Registered Pension Plan
RPS	Retirement Pension Supplement (QPP)
RRIF	Registered Retirement Income Fund
RRSP	Registered Retirement Savings Plan
TFSA	Tax-Free Savings Account
VA	Veterans Affairs
VAC	Veterans Affairs Canada
WVA	War Veterans Allowance
YMPE	Yearly Maximum Pensionable earnings

Bibliography

Biscott, Lynn. *The Boomers Retire: A Guide for Financial Advisors and Their Clients.* Carswell Legal Pubns; 2 edition (November 2010)

Dennis T. Guest. *The Emergence of Social Security in Canada*, 3rd Edition. University of Washington Press (December 2001)

Diamond, Daryl. *Your Retirement Income Blueprint: A Six-Step Plan to Design and Build a Secure Retirement.* Wiley; 1 edition (April 19, 2011)

Government of Canada. *The Old Age Security Act* (R.S.C., 1985, c. O-9).

Keats, Robert. *A Canadian's Best Tax Haven: The US.* Second Edition. Self-Counsel Press (March 2015)

Little, Bruce. *Fixing the Future: How Canada's Usually Fractious Governments Worked Together to Rescue the Canada Pension Plan.* University of Toronto Press, Scholarly Publishing Division (October 11, 2008)

Pape, Gordon. RRSPs: *The Ultimate Wealth Builder.* Penquin Group, (January, 2014)

Pape, Gordon. *The Ultimate TFSA Guide,* Penquin Group, 2009

Preteau, Angela. *Canadians & The IRS: What You Need to Know About Uncle Sam.* Knowledge Bureau Newsbooks (March 31, 2014)

[Task Force on Financial Literacy. Report of Recommendations on Financial Literacy. Government of Canada (December 2010)](http://www.financialliteracyincanada.com/canadians-and-their-money.html)

Index

Administration Offices.........97
   Quebec Pension Plan......99
   Service Canada Offices....97
   Veterans Affairs Canada. .99
Canada's public pension system...3
   Canada/Quebec Pension Plan..5
   Old Age Security Program.4
   Provincial Income Supplement Programs.........17, 101
   Veterans Affairs Canada Program............................7
Clawback............................54
CPP/QPP..............................5
   Claiming Strategies...........77
   Disability Benefit..............28
   Disability Benefit for Child 30
   Living abroad...................46
   Post-Retirement Benefits. 16
   Retirement Pension..........14
   Survivor Benefits..............38
   YMPE and Contribution Rates...................................6
CPP/QPP Disability Benefit ....28p.
   Benefits............................29
   Eligibility..........................29
CPP/QPP Disability Benefit for Child............................30
   Benefits............................31
   Eligibility..........................30
   How To Apply.................31
CPP/QPP Post-Retirement Benefits..............................16

   Benefits............................16
   Eligibility..........................16
   How To Apply.................17
CPP/QPP Retirement Pension 14
   Benefits............................15
   Eligibility..........................15
   How To Apply.................16
CPP/QPP Survivor Benefits. 38
   Benefits............................38
   Eligibility..........................38
   How To Apply.................39
   Lump-sum Death Benefit 38
   Pension for Dependent Children..........................38
   Pension for Surviving Spouse..............................38
Defined Benefit Pension Plan 63
Defined Contribution Pension Plan..................................64
Disability Pension.................28
   CPP/QPP Disability Benefit 28
   CPP/QPP Disability Benefit for Child..........................30
   Veterans Affairs Disability Pension............................29
   Veterans Affairs Disability Pension for Spouse and Child...............................31
Documents Required..........103
   Proof of Canadian Legal Status..............................103
   Proof of date of birth.....103

Proof of Residence History 104
Employer Pension Plans 63
　Converting Into Income. . 65
　Defined Benefit Pension Plan 63
　Defined Contribution Pension Plan 64
Family Benefits for the Disabled 30
　CPP/QPP Disability Benefit for Child 30
Family Benefits for the Low-Income Pensioners 20
　OAS Allowance 20
　War Veterans Allowance. 23
Income Splitting Strategies ... 79
Individuals With High Income 88
Individuals With Low Income 86
Living abroad 45
　Canada/Quebec Pension Plan 46
　OAS Allowance 46
　OAS Guaranteed Income Supplement 46
　OAS Pension 45
　Provincial Income Supplement Programs 46
　Veterans Affairs Canada Program 46
Non-Resident Withholding Tax 49
OAS Allowance 20
　Benefits 22
　Documents Required 22
　Eligibility 20
　How To Apply 22
　Living abroad 46
　OAS Recovery Tax 54

OAS Allowance for the Survivor 35
　Benefits 37
　Documents Required 37
　Eligibility 35
　How To Apply 37
　Living abroad 46
　OAS Recovery Tax 54
OAS Guaranteed Income Supplement 12
　Benefits 13
　Eligibility 12
　How To Apply 14
　Living abroad 46
　OAS Recovery Tax 54
OAS Pension 9
　Benefits 10
　Documents Required 12
　Eligibility 9
　How To Apply 11
　Living abroad 45
OAS Program 4
　Allowance for the Survivor 35
　OAS Guaranteed Income Supplement 12
　OAS Pension 9
OAS Recovery Tax 52
　Clawback on the GIS and the Allowance 54
　Non-Residents 53
Personal Tax Shelter 67
Provincial Income Supplement Programs 17, 101
　Alberta 17
　British Columbia 17
　Living abroad 46
　Manitoba 17
　New Brunswick 18
　Newfoundland and Labrador 18

Northwest Territories........18
Nova Scotia.....................18
Nunavut...........................18
Ontario............................17
Quebec/ Prince Edward Island....................................18
Saskatchewan..................17
Yukon.............................18
Registered Retirement Income Funds...............................69
Registered Retirement Savings Plan.............................67
Retirement Pension................9
   CPP/QPP Post-Retirement Benefits...........................16
   CPP/QPP Retirement Pension..................................14
   Family Benefits for the Low-Income Pensioners...20
   OAS Guaranteed Income Supplement......................12
   OAS Pension......................9
   Provincial Income Supplement Programs.................17
   War Veterans Allowance. 18
RRSP Withdrawal Strategies. 80
Savings and Investment Strategies.......................................82
Social Security Agreement...44
Survivor Benefits..................35
   CPP/QPP Survivor Benefits 38
   OAS Allowance for the Survivor................................35
   War Veterans Allowance. 39
Tax-Free Savings Accounts...69
Taxes.................................

Canadian Tax Treaty Countries..................................54
   Income Tax on Public Pension Benefits.....................48
   Non-Resident Withholding Tax................................49
   OAS Recovery Tax...........52
US Taxation...........................
   Complications..................93
   Income Tax.....................91
   Non-Resident's Withholding Tax...............................91
   OAS Recovery Tax...........92
   Registered Retirement Savings Plans.........................93
Veterans Affairs Canada Program...................................7
   Disability Pension............29
   Disability Pension for Spouse and Child.............31
   Living abroad..................46
   War Veterans Allowance. 39
Veterans Affairs Disability Pension...............................29
   Benefits...........................30
   Eligibility.........................29
   How to Apply.................30
Veterans Affairs Disability Pension for Spouse and Child 31
   Benefits...........................31
   Eligibility.........................31
   How to Apply.................32
War Veterans Allowance...18, 39
   Benefits...........................20
   Eligibility.........................19
   How to Apply...........20, 39

About the Author

Lee Tang is a retired executive of a major global insurance company. Prior to his retirement, he has worked as an actuary, a risk officer, and a chief financial officer for several major insurance organizations in the United States, Canada, and Taiwan.

Plea from the Author

Hey, Reader. So you got to the end of my book. I hope that means you enjoyed it. Whether or not you did, I would just like to thank you for giving me your valuable time to entertain you. I am blessed to have such a fulfilling job, but I have that job only because of people like you; people kind enough to give my books a chance and spend their hard-earned money buying them. For that, I am eternally grateful.

If you would like to discover more about my other books then please visit my website for full details. You can find it at:

Also feel free to contact me by email (leetang888@gmail.com), as I would love to hear from you.

If you enjoyed this book and would like to help, then you could think about leaving a review—even if it's only a line or two—on your favorite bookstore, Goodreads, or other sites; and talk about the book with your friends. The most important part of how well a book sells is how many positive reviews it has, so if you leave me one then you are directly helping me to continue this journey as a full-time writer. Thanks in advance to anyone who does. It means a lot.

Lee Tang

Also by Lee Tang

Standalones

Dual Momentum Trend Trading: *How to Avoid Costly Trading Mistakes and Make More Money in the Stock, ETF, Futures and Forex Markets with This Simple and Reliable Swing Trading Strategy.*

Canada's Public Pension System Made Simple: *The Secrets To Maximizing Your Retirement Income From Government Pensions*

Summary & Study Guide Series

1. **Summary & Study Guide - Brain Maker:** *The Power of Gut Microbes to Heal and Protect Your Brain-Including Diet Cheat Sheet*

2. **Summary & Study Guide - The Gene:** *An Intimate History*

3. **Summary & Study Guide - The Emperor of All Maladies:** *A Biography of Cancer*

4. **Summary & Study Guide - NeuroTribes:** *The Legacy of Autism*

5. **Summary & Study Guide - Brain Storms:** *The Race to Unlock the Secrets of Parkinson's Disease*

6. **Summary & Study Guide - The End of Diabetes:** *The Eat to Live Plan to Prevent and Reverse Diabetes-Including Diet Cheat Sheet*

7. **Summary & Study Guide - The End of Heart Disease:** *The Eat to Live Plan to Prevent and Reverse Heart Disease-Including Diet Cheat Sheet*

8. **Summary & Study Guide - ADHD Nation:** *Anatomy of An Epidemic - Attention-Deficit/Hyperactivity Disorder*

9. **Summary & Study Guide - The Obesity Code:** *Unlocking the Secrets of Weight Loss*

10. **Summary & Study Guide - How Not to Die:** *Discover the Foods Scientifically Proven to Prevent and Reverse Disease*

11. **Summary & Study Guide - Mind over Meds:** *Know When Drugs Are Necessary, When Alternatives Are Better - and When to Let Your Body Heal on Its Own*

12. **Summary & Study Guide - A Crack in Creation:** *Gene Editing and the Unthinkable Power to Control Evolution*

13. **Summary & Study Guide - The Gene Machine:** *How Genetic Technologies Are Changing the Way We Have Kids - and the Kids We Have*

14. **Summary & Study Guide - The Body Builders:** *Inside the Science of the Engineered Human*

15. **Summary & Study Guide - Into the Gary Zone:** *A Neuroscientist Explores the Border Between Life and Death*

16. **Summary & Study Guide - Fat for Fuel:** *A Revolutionary Diet to Combat Cancer, Boost Brain Power, and Increase Your Energy-Including Diet Cheat Sheet*

17. **Summary & Study Guide - The Alzheimer's Solution:** *A Breakthrough Program to Prevent and Reverse Cognitive Decline at Every Age*

18. **Summary & Study Guide - Healing Arthritis:** *Your 3-Step Guide to Conquering Arthritis Naturally*

19. **Summary & Study Guide - Rise of the Necrofauna:** *The Science, Ethics, and Risks of De-Extinction*

20. **Summary & Study Guide - We Are Our Brains:** *A Neurobiography of the Brain from the Womb to Alzheimer's*

21. **Summary & Study Guide - The Teenage Brain:** *A Neuroscientist's Survival Guide to Raising Adolescents and Young Adults*

22. **Summary & Study Guide - The Better Brain Solution:** *How to Reverse and Prevent Insulin Resistance of the Brain, Sharpen Cognitive Functions, and Avoid Memory Loss*

23. **Summary & Study Guide - The Plant Paradox:** *The Hidden Dangers in "Healthy" Foods That Cause Disease and Weight Gain*

24. **Summary & Study Guide - The Fountain:** *A Doctor's Prescription to Make 60 the New 30*

25. **Summary & Study Guide - Resurrection Science:** *Conservation, De-Extinction and the Precarious Future of Wild Things*

26. **Summary & Study Guide - Sapiens:** *A Brief History of Humankind*

27. **Summary & Study Guide - Homo Deus:** *A Brief History of Tomorrow*

28. **Summary & Study Guide - The Beautiful Cure:** *Harnessing Your Body's Natural Defences*

29. **Summary & Study Guide - The Diabetes Code:** *Prevent and Reverse Type 2 Diabetes Naturally*

30. **Summary & Study Guide - Brain Food:** *The Surprising Science of Eating for Cognitive Power*

31. **Summary & Study Guide - Anticancer Living:** *Transform Your Life and Health with the Mix of Six*

32. **Summary & Study Guide - The End of Epidemics:** *The Looming Threat to Humanity and How to Stop It*

33. **Summary & Study Guide - The Rise and Fall of the Dinosaurs:** *A New History of a Lost World*

34. **Summary & Study Guide - 10% Human:** *How Your Body's Microbes Hold the Key to Health and Happiness*

35. **Summary & Study Guide - The Mind-Gut Connection:** *How the Hidden Conversation Within Our Bodies Impacts Our Mood, Our Choices, and Our Overall Health*

36. **Summary & Study Guide - Civilization:** *The West and the Rest*

37. **Summary & Study Guide - Microbia:** *A Journey into the Unseen World Around You*

38. **Summary & Study Guide - An Elegant Defense:** *The Extraordinary New Science of the Immune System*

39. **Summary & Study Guide - Cancerland:** *A Medical Memoir on Cancer and Stem Cell Research*

40. **Summary & Study Guide - Empty Planet:** *The Shock of Global Population Decline*

41. **Summary & Study Guide - The Longevity Paradox:** *How to Die Young at a Ripe Old Age*

42. **Summary & Study Guide - Eat to Beat Disease:** *The New Science of How Your Body Can Heal Itself*

43. **Summary & Study Guide - The Tangled Tree:** *A Radical New History of Life*

44. **Summary & Study Guide – The Body:** *A guide for Occupants*

45. **Summary & Study Guide - The Spectrum of Hope:** *An Optimistic and New Approach to Alzheimer's Disease and Other Dementias*

46. **Summary & Study Guide - Memory Rescue:** *Supercharge Your Brain, Reverse Memory Loss, and Remember What Matters Most*

47. **Summary & Study Guide – The Longevity Code:** *Secrets to Living Well for Longer from the Front Lines of Science*

48. **Summary & Study Guide – Healing Anxiety and Depression**

49. **Summary & Study Guide - Healing ADD/ADHD:** *The Breakthrough Program that Allows You to See and Heal the 7 Types of ADD/ADHD*

50. **Summary & Study Guide - The Telomere Miracle:** *Scientific Secrets to Fight Disease, Feel Great, and Turn Back the Clock on Aging*

51. **Summary & Study Guide - The Finance Curse:** *How Global Finance Is Making Us All Poorer*

For a complete list of books by Lee Tang and information about the author, visit *https://lmtpress.wordpress.com.*

www.ingramcontent.com/pod-product-compliance
Lightning Source LLC
Chambersburg PA
CBHW030807180526
45163CB00003B/1181